God: The Holy Spirit

God: The Holy Spirit

The Conquering Power Within

R. C. JETTE

RESOURCE *Publications* · Eugene, Oregon

GOD: THE HOLY SPIRIT
The Conquering Power Within

Resource Publications
An Imprint of Wipf and Stock Publishers
199 W. 8th Ave., Suite 3
Eugene, OR 97401

www.wipfandstock.com

PAPERBACK ISBN: 978-1-7252-5636-1
HARDCOVER ISBN: 978-1-7252-5637-8
EBOOK ISBN: 978-1-7252-5638-5

All Scriptures are taken from the King James Version (KJV),
public domain.

Manufactured in the U.S.A.   NOVEMBER 11, 2019

This book is dedicated to my Lord and Savior, Jesus Christ!

I also dedicate it to my husband, Paul, for his continuous encouragement. My daughter, Dawn, for freeing me up to write.

I want to give a loving mention to my son, PJ and his daughter, Keira, my daughter, Christina, and her sons, Andrew, Matthew, Joshua, and her daughter, Sarah, who is with the Lord.

A special thanks is given to Wipf and Stock Publishers for their continued publication of my books. I thank their staff who have constantly made this challenge easier. I want to give special mention to Matthew Wimer, Daniel Lanning, George Callihan, and Shannon Carter to whom are more appreciated than my words can express.

Previously published by them through their Resource Publications:

Nonfiction:

1. *Storms Are Faith's Workout: Preparing Christians for Spiritual Ambush* (2018).

2. *Faith's Journey Confronts Obstacles: Instructing God's Soldiers to Overcome in His Armor* (2019).

3. *Satan's Strategy to Torment Through Physical Ambush: Educating God's Soldiers of Satan's Plot to Shatter Faith Through Sickness and Disease* (2019).

4. *Spiritual Shipwreck on the Horizon: Exhorting Christians to Contend for the Faith and Comprehend the Deceitfulness of Sin* (2019).

5. *Satan Has no Authority Over God's Soldier: Illuminating Godlike Faith* (2019).

Fiction:

1. *The Elfdins and the Gold Temple: An Oralee Chronicle* (2018).

2. *Charlie McGee and the Leprechaun: Life's Curious Twist of Events* (2019).

3. *The Shrines of Manitoba: Dark Secrets Shall Be Brought to Light* (2019).

And, behold, I send the promise of my Father upon you: but tarry ye in the city of Jerusalem, until ye be endued with power from on high.

−LUKE 24:49

Ye are of God, little children, and have overcome them: because greater is he that is in you, than he that is in the world.

−1 JOHN 4:4

He that overcometh shall inherit all things; and I will be his God, and he shall be my son.

−REVELATION 21:7

Contents

Introduction

I have previously written five books dealing with faith. When I finished the last one, I kept hearing in my spirit that God wants his children enlightened to the Holy Spirit. It seems we can't truly walk in conquering power without an understanding of the truth that this power comes from the Spirit of God.

Knowledge is the beginning of living in such power. The authority which has been given to us through Christ as revealed in my book, *Satan Has No Authority Over God's Soldier: Illuminating Godlike Faith*, is the foundation to walk in conquering power. However, that knowledge takes time to grasp hold of in our understanding. That's why I wrote *Storms Are Faith's Workout; Faith's Journey Confronts Obstacles; Satan's Strategy to Torment Through Physical Ambush;* and *Spiritual Shipwreck on the* Horizon to build up and strengthen our faith and prepare us for the fact that Satan doesn't have power or authority over us.

Unless God's soldiers comprehend that Godlike faith is vital in this warfare in which we partake of daily, we will never walk in the power dwelling in us through the Holy Spirit. We must believe in, trust in, and yield to the Spirit's guidance to live a victorious and conquering life.

Jesus is definitely the Son of God, but while He walked this earth, He was a man who walked in the power of the Holy Spirit. It was Christ's example that revealed to us what can be done if we deny our flesh and surrender our life to the Spirit.

I have mentioned this title to some people, and they were anticipating reading it. However, this book is not to hype anyone up. As a matter of fact, it's written to reveal who the Holy Spirit is, his work in God's soldiers, and how critically we need his baptism.

Each chapter will build upon the previous one until the last chapters bring forth our understanding of the indwelling power of the Holy Spirit. It's the truth of the Scriptures that must be revealed and comprehended. Conquering power is not bought for a song or through living a complacent and lethargic life. It's something that will be part of the lives of us who understand self-denial. Jesus made clear the requirement of following him is denying self and picking up our cross daily.

There seems to be much so-called Holy Spirit power out there. However, the lives of many claiming the Spirit's power are living in sins that will not inherit the kingdom of God. What is being exhibited is not Holy Spirit power. It's power, but not of God. This may offend some. But as I have stated before, my books are not for those desiring their ears to be tickled. I write for those who desire to hear, "Well done, thou good and faithful servant: thou hast been faithful over a few things, I will make thee ruler over many."

There's an incredible lack of knowledge in the church, as my previous books have exposed. The Holy Spirit is trying to awaken God's soldiers to the truth that we have the power to conquer the devil. We have allowed him to deceive us into accepting defeat, sin, sickness, disease, etc.. We must comprehend that Christ conquered the devil's power and authority through his shed blood on the cross of Calvary. All who are born again have been given that authority over all Satan's power except death.

This book is intended to build upon my other books and give revelation to the truth that we can live in Holy Spirit power above the problems, trials, storms, obstacles, strategies, etc. of Satan. He's been vanquished by Christ and no longer has any authority or power over us who are born again and are filled with the Holy Spirit. However, I must reiterate that it's necessary to understand this power comes at the cost of self-denial and being Christlike.

It's imperative that we be willing to hear what the Spirit is saying to the church. Too many have dogmatically or inflexibly wrapped themselves in their cocoon of dogma and are unwilling to allow the Holy Spirit to penetrate its shell. What I mean is that we follow whatever was taught to us by our parents, our preacher, our denomination, etc. When this happens, we dig a mote around that belief and will not allow any other thought to enter our mind. We become unteachable to the Holy Spirit.

This book is meant to open blinded eyes. God's soldiers must permit our hearts to become flesh and give place to the Holy Spirit to illuminate that He is God, that He indwells us, and that He is here to guide us into all truth. However, if we are unteachable, we will not be enlightened to truth.

We must realize this power was given to us because Christ paid the ultimate price of denying self. To be illuminated, we must deny self what we have dogmatically believed and be teachable. Unless we are willing to walk in the spirit and not the flesh, we will not live in the Spirit's power. This miraculous, conquering, enemy defeating ability is only achieved as we deny our flesh and yield to the Holy Spirit!

Chapter 1

A Divine Person

How much more shall the blood of Christ,
*who through the **eternal spirit** offered himself*
without spot to God, purge your conscience
from dead works to serve the living God?

–HEBREWS 9:14

I n order to walk in the conquering power of the Holy Spirit, it
must be established that He's a Divine Person. He's not a mere
influence of divine power. His Deity must be a revelation to us if
we are going to let him guide and direct our lives.

First of all, we need to look at some qualities or attributes of
the Holy Spirit that show He is God.

THE HOLY SPIRIT IS ETERNAL

In the beginning, God created the heaven and the earth.
And the earth was without form, and void; and darkness
was upon the face of the deep. And the Spirit of God
moved upon the face of the waters (Genesis 1:1-2).

This Scripture reveals the Holy Spirit was here in the beginning of the physical creation with God, the Father, being active in creation. According to Hebrews 9:14, He is the Eternal Spirit.

When we say the Holy Spirit is eternal or perpetual, it means He always was, is now, and ever shall be. God, the Holy Spirit had no beginning, and He will have no end.

THE HOLY SPIRIT IS OMNIPRESENT

> Whither shall I go from thy spirit? Or whither shall I flee from thy presence . . . (Psalm 139:7-19).

The Holy Spirit is revealed here as omnipresent or present everywhere at once. It's impossible to escape the presence of the Spirit of God, for He's everywhere. What a comforting thought that is. No matter where we are, the Holy Spirit is there.

It's truly reassuring to us, who desire God's will in every aspect of our life, to know, in all trials, God is with us. Yet, a backsliding Christian might move from the community or church where first touched by the Spirit of God, thinking to escape from the Holy Spirit's convicting power. Even if we change our environment, our circumstances, preachers, etc., we won't be able to rid our heart of the feeling of conviction. Wherever we flee, we will not escape the presence of the Holy Spirit, for He's there waiting for us. He's faithfully reproving of sin and pointing us toward Jesus Christ.

THE HOLY SPIRIT IS OMNISCIENT

> Who hath directed the Spirit of the Lord, or being his counsellor hath taught him? With whom took he counsel, and who instructed him, and taught him in the path of judgment, and taught him knowledge, and shewed to him the way of understanding? (Isaiah 40:13-14)

This Scripture shows that the Holy Spirit is all wise and all-knowing within himself. No one teaches, directs, counsels, or reveals anything to him. His wisdom cannot be increased, because He already knows all things. He is the Spirit of knowledge and wisdom.

The Spirit searches all things, yea, the deep things of God (1 Corinthians 2:10-11). That means the deep things of God are always open to the Holy Spirit who knows everything God the Father knows.

The deepest limits of knowledge are an open book to the Spirit of God. If God's soldiers want to know the things of God, to know what is the perfect will of God for our life, we must be guided by the Holy Spirit.

> I will instruct thee and teach thee in the way which thou
> shalt go: I will guide thee with mine eye (Psalm 32:8).

To guide us in the Greek is to counsel us. God promises to counsel or guide us if we allow him to lead us. We cannot expect to be led in the way we should go or led into God's will if we are led by anything or anyone except God's Spirit.

We can't know the things of God, unless the Holy Spirit leads and guides us. Only He knows all things from the beginning to the end, not us.

THE HOLY SPIRIT IS INFINITE

> Such knowledge is too wonderful for me; it is high, I cannot attain unto it (Psalm 139:6).

The Psalmist states that God's knowledge is too wonderful, so high he cannot attain it. He is claiming God's knowledge is infinite. It is limitless, endless, and impossible to measure. Whereas, our knowledge is finite. It is limited, restricted, and imperfect.

Let's understand our finite knowledge or understanding. No matter how many times we read the Bible, how much Bible education we have, how much we learn, how much we understand, we will never, in this life, know all about God. God in all his power is truly beyond our full comprehension. He is unlimited (infinite), whereas, we are limited (finite).

Since we will never attain the full knowledge of God, it is imperative to continuously yield to the Holy Spirit to keep growing in knowledge and wisdom of God. Only as we keep surrendering to the Spirit and keep reading and studying our bible, will we continually increase in the understanding of God.

THE HOLY SPIRIT IS OMNIPOTENT

> O thou that art named the house of Jacob, is the Spirit of the Lord straightened? Are these his doings? Do not my words do good to him that walketh uprightly? (Micah 2:7)

The word straightened means narrowed. It suggests being limited or restricted. The Spirit of God is not restricted by any outside force. He's all powerful. His power is seen both in the Creation and in his work in the world today.

The omnipotence of the Holy Spirit could cause some to wonder why He doesn't change things in this world. After all, He is omnipotent, He could do something about the problems that mankind face and experience.

He could do whatever He wanted. However, there is the factor of mercy to be considered. We must understand God's mercy mixed with his love and compassion. When the Holy Spirit does finally intrude to bring forth God's righteous Kingdom on earth, all problems will be Divinely removed. But at that moment, all second chances will be lost. In other words, there would be no more chance for salvation.

> The Lord is not slack concerning his promise, as some men count slackness; but is longsuffering to us-ward, not willing that any should perish, but that all should come to repentance (2 Peter 3:9).

The mercy involved in this means that judgment is currently being withheld. Because the Holy Spirit is omnipotent or all-powerful, He can control or limit his own power. He's not restricted in any way. It's impossible for him to be more powerful, yet, his full power is held back by himself.

> Who is a God like unto thee, that pardoneth iniquity,
> and passeth by the transgression of the remnant of his
> heritage? He **retaineth** not his anger forever, because he
> delighteth in mercy (Micah 7:18).

If He were to unleash his whole power to consume sin, not one
would survive. So, He is restricted by himself. It is his love, his
mercy, and his compassion that stand in the way of his judgment
for the time being.

Before we can truly understand that it's the Holy Spirit who
empowers us to live the conquering life, we must accept that He
is God indwelling us who are born again. Only as we recognize
him as a divine Person, are we enabled to understand that He is
just as much God as the Father and Jesus. In no way does He have
an inferior status in the Godhead. It's the Spirit who breathes life
into the word of God to reveal the depth of meaning. Until we are
immersed in him, we cannot fathom the deeper meanings of what
we read in the Bible.

Without fellowship with God the Holy Spirit, our life becomes dull, routine, negative, and lethargic. It's the Spirit who
gives us fresh insight and revelations of God and his word. Our
spirits are refreshed with living water and we find ourselves living
the abundant and conquering life no matter how severe the storm
or how difficult the obstacles (John 10:10). Through the Spirit's
revelation, we know that God, in the Person of the Holy Spirit, will
never leave us nor forsake us!

Chapter 2

The Paraclete

And I will pray the Father, and he shall give you another Comforter, that he may abide with you forever.

– JOHN 14:16

This chapter is meant to further explain that the Holy Spirit is God. He's here to convict of sin, to give glory to Christ, and to always direct us to Jesus.

Through the Holy Spirit's indwelling us, we are enabled to live a life that knows Satan has no power or authority over us. Without comprehending his divinity, we will not be enabled to yield to his conquering power. The power of Pentecost belongs to us, and it's time we fully understood the Paraclete and walked in his power.

To help us truly understand the Holy Spirit's work, I will, as usual, build upon each chapter to unfold the necessary foundation to leave no doubt as to who the Holy Spirit is, his power and ability, and the power that resides in us through him.

When Jesus called him another comforter. He was stating the Spirit will do in my absence what He would do if He were physically present with us. In other words, the Paraclete or Holy Spirit continues what Christ himself did while on earth. This implies that Jesus had been a Comforter to his disciples, and the Spirit will come to take his place and continue his ministry with his disciples.

As "another comforter," the Holy Spirit will be like Jesus in the disciples' lives. This means Jesus' work will not be broken off at his death and glorification, nor will the fellowship his disciples have known to be broken off upon his departure from them. He will continue both his work and his fellowship with his disciples through the person of the Holy Spirit.

The personality of the Holy Spirit is derived from the use of the personal pronouns in relation to him. The use of masculine pronoun "He" instead of it, reveals the Spirit is a person. In order to understand the biblical teachings on the Holy Spirit or Paraclete, it must be affirmed that He is a person.

> Even the Spirit of truth whom the world cannot receive, because it seeth him not, neither knoweth him; but ye know him; for he dwelleth with you, and shall be in you (John 14:17).

By the world, the Apostle John means those who are influenced only by the base desires of the lusts of the flesh, the lusts of the eyes, and the pride of life. These cannot receive the Spirit of truth, because they see him not, have no spiritual discernment, and follow the dictates of their corrupt passions and affections.

The Spirit's essential office is to manifest, vindicate, and apply the truth. In essence and in action the Holy Spirit is characterized by truth. He brings people to the truth of God. He's called the Spirit of truth because He is the Spirit of Jesus who is the truth (John 15:26, 16:13; 1 John 4:6, 5:6; John 14:6). As such, He bears witness to the truth, enlightens concerning the truth, exposes untruth, and guides the believer into all truth (John 18:37, 16:8, 16:13).

Jesus seemed to indicate a limited presence of the Holy Spirit prior to Pentecost, and then afterward in a fuller measure as Spirit-filled and Spirit-empowered witnesses. There is unquestionably an inner work of the Spirit of God in the Old Testament in the hearts of his people. However, it's clear that under the New Covenant, the work of the Spirit would involve a new inwardness.

> He that believeth on me, as the scripture hath said, out of
> his belly shall flow rivers of living water. (But this spake
> he of the Spirit, which they that believe on him should
> receive: for the Holy Ghost was not yet given; because
> that Jesus was not yet glorified (John 7:38-39).

The Holy Spirit will do a work within the hearts of the redeemed
that will go far beyond anything previously experienced. Because
of this new work within the hearts of men, they would be able to
impart streams of life-giving powers to others.

> But the comforter, which is the Holy Ghost, whom the
> Father will send in my name, he shall teach you all things,
> and bring all things to your remembrance, whatsoever I
> have said unto you (John 14:26).

The ministry of the Holy Spirit will include both recalling what
Jesus had taught and lead us into new areas of Divine truth in the
word. In other words, the ministry of the Spirit is predominantly
Christ-oriented, a part of which is to teach and remind us of what
Jesus taught in his word and to reveal revelations not seen before.
The Holy Spirit is never self-serving.

The Paraclete or Comforter is identified as the "Holy Spirit."
For the New Testament Christian, the most important thing about
the Spirit is not his power (Acts 1:8), but that He is **holy**. His holy
character, along with the manifestation of that holy character in
our lives is what matters most (Romans 1:4; Galatians 5:22-26).
It's only through his influence that we can live a holy life. Without
holiness, no man/woman shall see the Lord (Hebrews 12:14).

If there is anything not understood or unknown, the Paraclete will give understanding. The inspiration of the Holy Spirit enabled the disciples to not only give a true history of Christ's death,
life, and resurrection, but also gave them the most impeccable
recollection of all the words which He had spoken to them. This
enabled them to transmit to future generations the words Jesus
uttered in his sermons, and his different discourses with them, the
Jews, and others.

Because of this attribute of the Holy Spirit, God's soldiers are able to recollect the words of Christ written in the Scriptures, and to understand their meaning. As we study the Bible, we can trust the Paraclete to plant truth in our mind, convince us of God's will, and remind us when we stray from it.

Let me clarify that the Paraclete (Holy Spirit) will not make revelations of new notions. He only brings to our remembrance or illuminates what Christ has said in his word, and what was before in the word revealed. There are NO new truths outside of the written word, but new discoveries of old truths in the word of God not yet apprehended.

The Paraclete is to teach. This means He is our teacher. Because the Bible is a spiritual book, we need someone to teach us its meaning. We cannot comprehend spiritual truths without it being spiritually discerned by the Holy Spirit.

When the Holy Spirit reminds us, it not only includes what has been previously mentioned, but it also involves any special promise the Lord has given us in the past. It's the faithfulness of the Paraclete to remind us of God's word, his promises, his will, etc. that encourages us in the trials of this life.

> But when the comforter is come, whom I will send unto you from the Father, even the Spirit of truth, which proceedeth from the Father, he shall testify of me (John 15:26).

The Holy Spirit testifies or gives witness of Christ. He leads into a greater apprehension of gospel truths. Any witness contrary to Scripture bears witness to falsehood and is not led by the Holy Spirit. As the Spirit of truth, He will suggest true reasoning to our minds and true courses of action for our life.

He is the Comforter whom has been sent by Jesus and the Father. Because He is a Person, He can be grieved (Ephesians 4:30) and sinned against (Mark 3:29). This depicts the Holy Spirit is not a mere personal power or influence. Because he proceeds from the Father, it implies He is part of the Father as light is part of the sun. As Christ and the Father are one (John 10:30), so is the Spirit who

issues forth from the Father, one with the Father and Son. Therefore, the Paraclete is not only a Person, but He is as much God as
the Father and the Son.

> And when he is come, he will reprove the world of sin,
> and of righteousness, and of judgment (John 16:8).

When the Holy Spirit came on the day of Pentecost, He, by his
inward operation in men's hearts and by his gifts bestowed upon
believers reproved the world. His principal relation to witnessing
and proclaiming the gospel will be to "reprove." The Greek term
means to convict, expose, refute, and convince.

It is most difficult to impress man of sin, righteousness, and
judgment, because he can always attempt to justify himself by as-
serting an inexcusable motive for sin. How many times have we
heard people justify themselves by claiming that was not what was
meant? How many times have we heard someone claim that it's no
big deal? How many times have we heard someone accuse others
of taking things too seriously? How many times have we heard
someone claim others expect more from them than God does?
How many times have we been accused of not loving because we
point out sin?

The Paraclete convinces of sin and calls us to repentance,
shows the standard of God's righteousness, and demonstrates
Christ's judgment over Satan. This conviction is the Divine meth-
od of conquering the veil Satan has cast over the mind of each
unregenerate person (2 Corinthians 4:3–4).

The fact that Satan has been judged (defeated) proves the
solemn certainty of judgment. The cross and the empty tomb have
shown Christ as victor. Because of Christ, the ruler of this world
(Satan) and those who follow him have been defeated and con-
demned (judged).

> Howbeit when he, the Spirit of truth is come, he will
> guide you into all truth; for he shall not speak of himself;
> but whatsoever he shall hear, that shall he speak: and he
> will shew you things to come (John 16:13).

The position within the heart of the believer which the Paraclete now occupies secures the closest relationship, so that He, the Spirit himself, is able to create impressions within our consciousness which seem to have occurred only to our own finite mind. All spiritual truth must be imparted by the indwelling Spirit in this way.

The truth into which the Holy Spirit guides is the truth about Christ. He also helps us through patient practice to discern right from wrong. He guides us into the truth of God's word, revealing the hidden meaning, making its teachings clear.

It must be comprehended anything not in keeping with the teachings of Jesus and the written word of God is not guided by the Spirit. In other words, any so called "new" movement of the Holy Spirit where Christ's teachings are said to be outdated, overruled by new revelations, or that we no longer need the Bible is NOT of the Paraclete. The Holy Spirit has no independent teachings contrary to those of Jesus or the word of God.

He is the Spirit of truth, and as such, He will bear witness to the truth of Jesus, will lead us into a greater revelation of redemptive truth, and interpret the meaning of Scriptures. This means the Holy Spirit will lead us into a fuller revelation of the mind of God in redemption.

The Holy Spirit will witness to those who will hear, as to what lies ahead for the world and the church, making the prophetic Scriptures clear (Amos 3:7; Genesis 18:17). The Paraclete will not only reveal the prophetic events of the end time, but to the events yet future in the experience of believers. Many times God makes known certain things that lie ahead and prepares the individual believer for unforeseen eventualities.

> He shall glorify me: for he shall receive of mine, and shall
> shew it unto you (John 16:14).

The Holy Spirit's ministry is to call attention to the one whom He represents; He reveals the things of Christ. The Spirit draws no attention to himself, but promises the glory of Christ. The Spirit's work is recognized by the glory given to Christ. If Christ is not being glorified, then it is not the Holy Spirit that is leading.

Let me clarify this important point, the Holy Spirit gives glory to Christ. Since the Holy Spirit's work exalts Christ, if we draw attention to ourselves, our ministry, etc. we are not being led by the Holy Spirit. If we are led of the Paraclete, our life, our words, our actions, our thoughts, etc. will give glory to Christ.

The Holy Spirit works within us to do what is necessary to awaken and deepen our awareness of Jesus' presence in our lives, drawing our hearts toward him in faith, love, obedience, communion, worship, and praise. He glorifies Christ in all He does. The Holy Spirit exalts Christ by reminding us of what is in the Scriptures and by giving us a deeper appreciation for him and his work.

The more we yield to the Holy Spirit, He will make us Christlike. True ministry in the Holy Spirit never serves a private or personal agenda. As he works in us and through us, the Paraclete continuously glorifies Christ who glorifies the Father.

What all this is conveying to us is that the Holy Spirit is God in us. He is not here to glorify himself or to cause us to glorify our ministry, our calling, etc. His work is to enable us to live in his conquering power. However, that cannot be accomplished unless we are in a right relationship with the Lord. Jesus walked in such power because He denied his body (flesh) and would not allow it to yield to the lusts of the flesh, the lusts of the eyes, and the pride of life. The less we yield to our flesh and the more we yield to the Paraclete or the Holy Spirit, He will have us walking in the conquering power that's our inheritance from Jesus!

Chapter 3

Pentecost Has Come

Tarry ye in the city of Jerusalem, until ye be endued with power from on high

—LUKE 24:49.

And, being assembled together with them, commanded them that they should not depart from Jerusalem, but wait for the promise of the Father, which, saith he, ye have heard of me.

—ACTS 1:4

And when the day of Pentecost was fully come, they were all with one accord in one place. And suddenly there came a sound from heaven as of a rushing mighty wind, and it filled all the house where they were sitting. And there appeared unto them cloven tongues like as of fire, and it sat upon each of them. And they were all filled with the Holy

Ghost, and began to speak with other tongues,
as the Spirit gave them utterance.

−ACTS 2:1-4

T his chapter, although short, is meant to refute a fallacy in some Pentecostal teachings about the Holy Spirit baptism. I believe the teaching of waiting or tarrying today for the Holy Spirit is conceived or devised by Satan to prohibit many from receiving the Spirit's conquering power. The sad truth is Christians are beguiled by the tarry mentality.

Furthermore, some are told they cannot get the baptism until this or that gets out of their life. This mentality is nothing but hogwash. Without the Holy Spirit, we will never get something out of our life. I will make this clear as we go along.

Let's look at the Holy Spirit baptism scripturally. First of all the one-hundred-twenty tarrying in Jerusalem were not waiting because they had to get themselves ready to receive him. They were not preparing themselves. They were in obedience to Jesus to tarry until they had been endued with power from on high.

The only reason they were waiting is because they were waiting for the Day of Pentecost which is fifty days after Passover. Pentecost doesn't come before then, and the Holy Spirit baptism would not be given until then. All God does is always in the fulness of his time (Galatians 4:4).

Hear me, the Scripture doesn't read, *and when they were ready.* It says, *and when the day of Pentecost was fully come.* It's absurd to think waiting for the Holy Spirit will get us ready for it. There is only one way to be ready to receive the Holy Spirit baptism and that's through a genuine salvation experience. There is nothing, outside of having accepted Jesus as our Savior, that we can do to make ourselves ready to receive the baptism of the Spirit.

> The blood of Jesus Christ his Son cleanseth us from all sin (1 John 1:7).

If we are blood washed, we are ready right now for the Holy Spirit baptism. Acts 10:44-46 reveals Cornelius and his household were not only saved, but filled with the Holy Spirit almost at the same time. This also refutes another false teaching that in order to be saved, we must be baptized in water.

> That if thou shalt confess with thy mouth the Lord Jesus, and shalt believe in thine heart that God hath raised him from the dead, thou shalt be saved. For with the heart man believeth unto righteousness; and with the mouth confession is made unto salvation (Romans 10:9-10).

Salvation is a matter of faith and faith alone. To claim water baptism is essential to salvation is teaching works and not faith.

The Holy Spirit in Acts 10:45 reveals the Spirit is a gift. God already gave the gift of the Holy Spirit on the Day of Pentecost. Just as salvation is a gift already given by Christ's sacrifice on the cross. God does not have to send Christ to Calvary again for us to be saved. It is just a matter of our receiving his gift of salvation (John 1:12).

God does not have to send the Holy Spirit again for us to have the baptism. All we have to do is receive the gift of the Holy Spirit. In Acts 19:1-6, Paul didn't ask them if God gave them the Holy Spirit, but he asked if they had **received** him. Then in Acts 8:14-15, Peter and John didn't pray for God to give the people in Samaria the Holy Spirit. They didn't ask God to pour out his Spirit on them, They prayed that they might **receive** the Holy Spirit.

All this also refutes the teaching that we receive the baptism at salvation. We receive the Holy Spirit, but not the baptism at salvation. These were disciples of Jesus Christ. In Samaria, they were saved and had been baptized in the Name of Jesus Christ, but had not received the baptism in the Holy Spirit with the evidence of speaking with tongues until sometime after their conversion. It is a separate act of grace. The reason Cornelius and his house were baptized in the Spirit at salvation was to show the Jews that God was going to baptize any and all who believed in Jesus as savior. Furthermore, how did the Jews know Cornelius and the others had received the baptism? Because they heard them speaking in tongues (this is the initial evidence of the baptism of the Holy Spirit) and magnifying God (Acts 10:46).

> For by grace are ye saved through faith; and that not of yourselves: it is the gift of God: Not of works, lest any man should boast (Ephesians 2:8-9).

We don't earn salvation and we don't earn the Holy Spirit Baptism. Both are the gifts of God to his children. It's just a matter of receiving them by faith.

If some who are born again, are reading this, and have not received the Holy Spirit baptism, it's not because we have to clean up. Without the Holy Spirit's conquering power, we are powerless to conquer or overcome this life.

Salvation is the only requirement. Once saved, He is waiting for us to ask for him. As soon as we ask, we just receive. Our speaking with other tongues is our evidence that we have been baptized in God's Spirit. It's the same that we did at salvation, we recognized we were a sinner, asked to be forgiven, asked Jesus to save us, and we received his gift of salvation.

To teach that we have to do something other than receive by faith Christ as Savior or do something other than receive by faith the Holy Spirit baptism is combining works and unbelief. Neither salvation or the Holy Spirit baptism is earned, worked for, or waiting for us to clean up. They are gifts from a loving Heavenly Father to God's children who believe him to give salvation and the Holy Spirit baptism. Luke 11:13 illuminates our heavenly Father will give the Holy Spirit to us when we ask. For He knows we are not capable of conquering this life without the power of the Holy Spirit.

The Holy Spirit came on the Day of Pentecost, we do not have to tarry or wait for him to come. He's here and waiting for every born-again believer to receive him. It's a matter of receiving him by faith as we received salvation by faith. We ask him to fill us, and He will!

Chapter 4

The Outpouring of the Holy Spirit

And it shall come to pass afterward, that I will pour out my spirit upon all flesh; and your sons and your daughters shall prophesy, your old men shall dream dreams, your young men shall see visions: And also upon the servants and upon the handmaids in those days will I pour out my spirit. And it shall come to pass, that whosoever shall call on the name of the Lord shall be delivered.

—JOEL 2:28,29,32

In this chapter, we must grasp that the Day of Pentecost was only the beginning of the outpouring of the Holy Spirit. It was not the end, but the introduction of the Spirit's baptism of power.

Throughout the Old Testament, God's continuing goal is to share his presence with his people. We see this from Creation through the Exodus and beyond. As a matter of fact, we are told in the Garden, God used to come down and visit with Adam and Eve in the cool of the day (Genesis 3:8). In other words, God Almighty came to fellowship with his creation.

God hasn't changed. It's man who altered when he switched fathers in the Garden of Eden. Sin chose Satan and man became his slave. Now, we are out of fellowship with God until we are born again. Once we are in a right relationship with God, He once again comes down in the cool of the day (so to speak) to fellowship with us.

In the Old Testament, we find very few the Holy Spirit came upon. Those few were a small minority in ratio to his people. God desires to endow all his people with his power, not just a handful. That's why Joel prophesied a day when God would pour out his Spirit on **all** those "who call upon the Name of the Lord."

The Spirit would pour out like a rain fall, or waterfall. No longer would it be drop by drop like in the Old Covenant. God's intimate presence with his people began on the day of Pentecost. Here me, it was only the beginning, the start, etc. On that day began the new relationship between God and his people.

Pentecost is an *outpouring*. This implies great abundance and fullness. We must realize that the outpouring of the Holy Spirit and the accompanying supernatural signs cannot be limited to just the one day of Pentecost.

It was partially accomplished at Pentecost, which was merely the inception. We cannot limit the Spirit's power or confine it to a once happening. In other words, it was not a once and for all occurrence in church history. It will continue to flow **until** the wonders in the heavens and in the earth are shown (Acts 2:30).

The full realization of this outpouring of the Holy Spirit will one day be followed by the end time cosmic signs and the "day of the Lord" as described in Matthew 24 and the book of Revelation.

Pentecost was not the fulfillment of the prophecy. Thus, the outpouring will continue as long as this world lasts. This is seen when Peter asserted the prophecy to be parallel with the Divine calling of salvation. The outpouring and salvation are to run side by side throughout the whole Christian dispensation. Peter stressed this truth when he claimed the promise is unto us, and to our children, and to all that are afar off, even as many as the Lord our God shall call (Acts 2:39).

It has been too much the habit with God's soldiers to rest satisfied with a very partial and moderate fulfillment of the promise of the Spirit. We should be expecting an outpouring. It's a blessing that we should expect. Why does it seem so limited?

Let me explain why. It's because we have limited the overflow in our life. It's time to remove the hindrances that stand in the way or are prohibiting such an outpouring of the Spirit in our lives. The unholiness which exists in the church. Ignorance and misapprehension regarding the work of the Spirit have limited his flow in the lives of believers.

The personal responsibility of all Christians in relation to the extension of God's Kingdom is not felt as it should be. There's too much limitation, by man. We hinder him and wonder why we're not walking in conquering power.

Joel revealed the "outpouring" would be "upon all flesh." This is talking about mankind and not animals. This refers to every class of people, not every individual. Salvation is desired by God for all men (2 Peter 3:9). However, not all men will be saved.

What Joel was revealing in this coming manifestation of the Spirit is that there will be no distinction made on the grounds of sex, nationality, age, or position (Galatians 3:28).

1. The outpouring would be *without National distinction*, for there is neither Jew nor Greek.

2. It will be *without social distinction*, for there is neither bond nor free.

3. It will be *without sexual distinction*, for there is neither male nor female.

4. It will be *without ceremonial distinction*, for there is neither circumcision nor uncircumcision.

5. It will be *without intellectual or educational distinction*, for the Barbarian and even the Scythian (the lowest type of Barbarian) are free to share the blessing.

In other words, it would not be confined within the narrow bounds of Judea, not limited to one, but extended to all races. Not only adults, but children can receive this gift. Not only men, but women are recipients of this Holy Spirit outpouring.

The promise was implying something extraordinary and unexpected. The Spirit would burst through every barrier and quicken the energies of life in all classes. Spiritual light would not be confined to a select few.

Under the Old Covenant, only men were to preach and teach. However, when God poured out his Spirit in the New Covenant, it will be men and women (sons and daughters or male and female) who would prophesy.

1. Prophesy means to speak or sing by inspiration.

2. Prophet is an inspired man. He is one that prophesies.

3. Prophetess is the female of prophet. She is an inspired woman that prophesies.

Jesus stated that any who had ears to hear would hear. In other words, if we want to hear truth, we will receive truth whether it comes through Jew, Gentile, rich, poor, male, female, educated, uneducated.

I am not trying to convince of female preachers. I believe Jesus made that quite clear after his resurrection in John 20:17: *Jesus saith unto her, Touch me not, for I am not yet ascended to my Father: but **go** to my brethren, and **say** unto them, I ascend unto my Father, and your Father, and to my God, and your God.*

Mary Magdalene is the first one Jesus appeared to after his resurrection and she is the first one sent to preach his resurrection (Luke 16:9; John 20:18). Truth is truth no matter if it is accepted or not.

Joel is making it known long before it happened what to expect. In other words, know when the Spirit's outpouring comes, it will be on men and women. He said to expect your men and women to prophesy, to preach, to exhort, to instruct, and to teach.

What is this Pentecost? What is this outpouring? First of all, we know the word Pentecost means fiftieth. Exodus 23:16 called the "The Feast of Harvest." In Exodus 34:22 it is called "The day of the first fruits."

The celebration of Pentecost was observed fifty days after the Sabbath of the Passover. It was celebrating the first fruits. Hear me now, when we receive our Pentecost experience, it's only receiving the first fruits. It's not to stop. It's not just one infilling. It's supposed to be like a rainfall or a waterfall.

When we think of Niagara Falls, it's like a gushing of water over those falls. That's what the baptism in the Holy Spirit is supposed to be like in our lives. If it's not falling continuously, it's because we have stopped the fall or flow.

Listen to me, we are so easily discontented. I don't know how many times I've heard children say they are bored. It seems like some of God's soldiers do the same. How can we be bored, if we're spending time with the Lord? We cannot be spending time with Jesus, if we're bored.

Sin in the church, iniquity in the lives of Christians has caused the waterfall to either stop or trickle. We cannot live the empowered life in the Spirit that God desires of us on just a trickle. We claim we don't have time to read our Bible, pray, etc., but we can watch television, play games, etc.

The early church walked in the power of the Holy Spirit because they prayed without ceasing. They were too content in the things of God to be malcontent. It's time for us to repent of our lackadaisical Christianity.

A Christian who has time to be bored is troubling. We need to covet the things of God, so the waterfall just keeps refreshing and refreshing us. Then and only then, will we have the power we need to conquer this life of sin.

Pentecost is the beginning of the life in the miraculous. However, none of us should covet the baptism in the Holy Ghost because of miraculous power. It should be coveted because it's the gift of enlightenment enabling us to understand the things of God.

When I was first saved, I comprehended the word of God to a degree. But after the baptism in the Spirit, it was like I went from using a flashlight to a flood light. It was like washing in a bucket to washing in the ocean. The flow of enlightenment is unlimited.

That which began at Pentecost has not ceased, and will continue right up to Christ's second advent. Hear me, the baptism in the Holy Spirit should be like Spring in the Christians life. Winter is past and flowers begin sprouting. The grass turns green and trees blossom. In other words, the Christian's life should start to really bring forth fruit of the Holy Spirit.

Many Christians receive the baptism in the Spirit and think we have it all now. Let me shed some light on this thought. We will NEVER have it all in this life. When we receive the baptism in the Spirit, we are only at the beginning of the conquering power God desires to surge through our life!

Chapter 5

Spirit of Power

But ye shall receive power, after that the Holy Ghost is come upon you: and ye shall be witnesses unto me both in Jerusalem, and in all Judea, and in Samaria, and unto the uttermost part of the earth.

−ACTS 1:8

Endowment with power by the Holy Spirit in the life of God's soldiers cannot be overemphasized. The degree of our light in this world is determined by whether or not we have been baptized in the Spirit.

Once we're born again, there is much potential or use for the Kingdom of God in our lives. If we're saved without the baptism in the Spirit, we're like the 15 watt bulb. If we're saved with the baptism in the Spirit, we're like the 1500 watt bulb.

The word power in Acts 1:8 is the Greek word *Dunamis*. It's the word from which we derive our word dynamite. The Holy Spirit gives us dynamic or vibrant power to live a conquering and victorious life.

So many Christians seem to be seeking more power or whatever to conquer. If we have the Holy Spirit baptism, we have all the power we'll ever need or will ever have in this life to conquer. Understand this truth, the Holy Spirit is the source of ALL power. We don't need more power, we need to decrease and let him increase. The more we yield to him, the more we walk in his power.

If we don't turn on the electricity to give power to the light-bulb, there's no light. Well, if we don't yield to the Holy Spirit, there's no power flowing through our life to be a light in this dark world.

> Ye are of God, little children, and have overcome them: because greater is he that is in you, than he that is in the world (1 John 4:4).

Our problem for a lack of power is that we don't cooperate with the Holy Spirit who lives in us. The power of the Spirit IN us is greater, more powerful than the devil. He's the conquering power that enables us to prevail over Satan and any of his diabolical plots, storms, schemes, obstacles, etc.

Just because we don't feel any power doesn't mean we don't have the power. Sometimes we may not feel saved, but it doesn't mean we're not saved. As God's soldiers, we don't go by what we feel, for we walk by faith, not by sight, or by feelings (2 Corinthians 5:7).

Many years ago, R. W. Schambach sent me a card with these words: **"The Greatest power ever known is inside me."** I don't know how many times while going through various storms, I would look at that card. When I quote it, it does something in me. Each time, the Holy Spirit would quicken me to 2 Timothy 1:6-7: *Wherefore I put thee in remembrance that thou stir up the gift of God, which is in thee by the putting on of my hands. For God hath not given us the spirit of fear, but of power, and of love, and of a sound mind.*

God wants us to stir up the gift of the Holy Spirit in us and to remember He is the Spirit of power. The greatest power in the Universe resides in us who are born-again and have received the Holy Spirit baptism. It's time for God's soldiers to believe what the word of God says, regardless of how we feel.

> So then faith cometh by hearing, and hearing by the
> word of God (Romans 10:17).

Now, if faith comes by hearing the word, then unbelief must come by believing what we feel. What is feeling? It is the voice of self, whereas, faith is the voice of the Spirit.

The voice of flesh, self, the old nature will say to forget it, it's just no use. We can't do this or conquer that. Yet, the voice of the Holy Spirit will say that with God NOTHING shall be impossible (Luke 1:27).

> But the hour cometh, and now is, when the true worship-
> pers shall worship the Father in spirit and in truth: for
> the Father seeketh such to worship him (John 4:23.

God wants us to listen to his word. We must understand if we walk in the Spirit, we won't go by feelings. We cannot be a conquering Christian if we walk by emotions. Why is that so? Because what we feel is the voice of the flesh. If we walk by our feelings, our emotions, our moods, etc. we are dominated by the old nature which has no ability to live in the conquering power of the Holy Spirit.

If we walk in the flesh, we walk by sight and not by faith. Because the Holy Spirit in us walks by faith and not by sight, it's in complete opposition to our flesh (Galatians 5:17). The greatest power in us is not our flesh. If we want to live a conquering, fuel filled life, it's time to understand that the greatest power in the Universe (the power that spoke all things into existence) resides in us. We must stop ambling a powerless walk and learn to advance in the Holy Spirit of power!

Chapter 6

Holy Spirit's Reconstructive Work

In the beginning God created the heaven and the earth. And the earth was without form, and void; and darkness was upon the face of the deep. And the Spirit of God moved upon the face of the waters.

–GENESIS 1:1-2

Thou sendest forth thy Spirit, they are created: and thou renewest the face of the earth.

–PSALM 104:30

I n this chapter, we will reveal the Holy Spirit in his reconstructive position in the Godhead. An understanding of his ability will help us to understand just how powerful He is.

The Bible introduces the Spirit at the very beginning in Genesis chapter 1. The first sentence states that God created the heaven and the earth. Then in the second sentence it states the earth was without form and void, and darkness was upon the face of the deep. Then in the third, we are told the Spirit of God moved upon the face of the waters.

Now, we know whatever God creates is invariably good. How then is there a chaotic earth in Genesis? What we have to understand is between the statement "in the beginning God created the heaven and the earth," and the statement "the earth was without form and void; and darkness was upon the face of the deep," something happened.

A part of God's creation involved angels which included the great and mighty archangel, Lucifer. However, this super angel's heart was lifted up in pride because of his beauty. Satan was God's most beautiful creation. He corrupted his wisdom by reason of his brightness (Ezekiel 28:17).

Before his fall, Lucifer was beautiful, righteous, and followed the Lord. Ezekiel 28:12 says: *sealest up the sum*. This means that nothing more could possibly be added to enhance his perfection. He had everything associated with greatness. However, he fell, and when he fell utter chaos followed.

So, between the two sentences in Genesis 1:1–2 is when Satan fell. Let's face it, how else could anything that God created be void and have darkness upon it? God is not associated with darkness (1 Thessalonians 5:5).

It is Satan who delights in darkness. Everything and everyone he touches is entangled with emptiness and darkness. He is the thief that steals, kills, and destroys (John 10:10).

Okay, that's enough about Satan's fall. We need to look at the Holy Spirit. He's not simply some "general power" surrounding the earth. While being personally meek, it must be understood the Holy Spirit knows no bounds. When exercising the power of God, there's no limit or maximum to the power of the Spirit.

> But ye shall receive power, after that the Holy Ghost is come upon you: and ye shall be witnesses unto me both in Jerusalem, and in all Judaea, and in Samaria, and unto the uttermost part of the earth (Acts 1:8).

The Holy Spirit is actually the dynamo, the generator, the power source of the Godhead. However, the power the Holy Spirit gives to us, while powerful, is limited. He could never trust fallible man with unlimited power.

The power of the Holy Spirit is an explosive power, a great and mighty power. It's the power within us that enables us to conquer the powers of Hell. No power of the devil can disable the power of the Spirit of God.

Let's take a closer look at the intention of this chapter to see what I believe God desires us to understand about the Spirit's reconstructive work.

We see that in Genesis chapter 1, the Holy Spirit's power was involved in creation throughout the creative and recreative process. He moved upon the face of this chaotic world to put into effect the creative word of God through Jesus Christ.

He carried out the organization process of assembling, structuring, sorting, and balancing all the elements. It was the Holy Spirit who did the actual nuts and bolts work of restoring order to the world and the Universe put in disarray by Satan.

The Holy Spirit was the construction foreman on the great work of redevelopment and recreation. It was no problem for him, the Spirit of God, to bring the dry land out of the chaos or to cause the waters to recede.

It's no problem for him to bring the new creation out of the old creation, or to develop or construct order in our lives from the disorder we had. The Holy Spirit has the power and the ability to change our chaotic life into a life of harmony.

That's why we have to allow the Spirit of God to do his reconstructive work in our lives. As we allow him to do it, He recreates us from the old nature which is created in the image of Satan and transforms us into the new nature which is created in the image of Christ Jesus.

My husband, when he was coming to the Lord, was shown that he had this big hole (a void) in his chest, and knew it was why he felt something was missing in his life. As he accepted Jesus as his savior, he sensed the void disappearing. As it vanished, he felt a sense of love and life which overwhelmed him, and he cried that he would die for Jesus. Of course, he learned later the Lord wants him to live for him.

We are the new creation in Christ Jesus because of the reconstructive work of the Holy Spirit working in us. He took all our confusion and chaos and transformed us into a life of harmony and order.

The Holy Spirit's reconstructive, regenerative, restoration, remaking, etc. work in us is the same power that transformed the chaotic creation in Genesis into an orderly creation. We can see our life before He began his renovation in us. We were without form and void and darkness ruled in us. The Spirit brought light into our life and began his reconstructive work to transform us from the darkness that ruled into God's marvelous light transforming us into the image of Christ. As we allow him freedom to work in us, He will reconstruct our life of chaos into something harmonious for the Lord!

Chapter 7

Fruit of the Spirit

But the fruit of the Spirit is love, joy, peace, long-suffering, gentleness, goodness, faith, meekness, temperance: against such there is no law.

–GALATIANS 5:22-23

In this chapter, understanding the fruit of the Spirit is vital in order to walk in conquering power. When fruit is abundantly flourishing in our life, we have learned to deny self. Fruit cannot grow where flesh (old nature) is predominant. Likewise, the works of the flesh cannot prosper where the fruit of the Spirit dominates.

Through the Holy Spirit, God's soldiers are enabled to conquer and break the power of sin in our life. The fruit of the Spirit is the spontaneous working of the Spirit within us. As we yield and obey him, He reconstructs us to replace our self-life or old nature with the Christ-life or Christlikeness. As this occurs, the more godly becomes our character.

Jesus made bearing fruit of the utmost importance in his teachings. Fruitfulness is something God's soldiers have to perceive if we are going to walk in his conquering power.

According to Galatians 5:17, the greatest struggle within ourselves is the battle between the flesh (old nature or self) and the spirit (new nature). If the flesh wins, it will become the controlling force in our life. The reality of the flesh ruling is that we bear no fruit and cannot walk in the Spirit's conquering power. If we yield to the Holy Spirit, we become Christ-centered, manifest the fruit of the Spirit, and live in his conquering power.

> Blessed is the man that walketh not in the counsel of the ungodly, nor standeth in the way of sinners, nor sitteth in the seat of the scornful. But his delight is in the law of the Lord; and in his law doth he meditate day and night. And he shall be like a tree planted by the rivers of water, that bringeth forth his fruit in his season; his leaf also shall not wither; and whatsoever he doeth shall prosper (Psalm 1:1-3).

The priority we give the word of God in our lives will determine the degree of our fruitfulness. As we abide in Christ, remain obedient to his word, and remain dependent on our relationship with him, God, the Holy Spirit will work in us, create, and produce the fruit of the Spirit.

Just because we have been baptized in the Spirit doesn't mean that we have automatic fruit. I don't know how many times through the years I have encountered unenlightened believers who believe the baptism means we've arrived. We use the gifts in every service like Mr. and Mrs. Christianity. Yet, our lives are living like the devil. Very fleshly, foul mouthed, fighting all the time with our spouse. Just plain works of the flesh individuals bearing no visible fruit of the Spirit.

When we walk in obedience to truth instead of obeying our flesh, the Holy Spirit transforms us, and we begin to bring forth his fruit by his power. That's why there were many times when teaching about the Holy Spirit, I was led to avoid the gifts. The Lord impressed me that, "too many are seeking my gifts and are withering." *He told me his children must bear fruit so that pride won't control the gifts.*

That truth put such Holy Spirit fear in me when I was a young Christian, that I avoided the gifts and concentrated on being a fruit bearer. I figured the fruit would make me more like Christ. If and when He believed it was time for me to function in the gifts, I was in no hurry. Like I said, I saw too many Christians puffed up in the gifts and their lives were no different than what they were before being saved.

The Lord made obvious that the gifts do not and never will produce holiness in our life. Only the fruit of the Spirit produces the holiness necessary to see God (Hebrews 12:14). Although the gifts of the Spirit are useful and helpful to the church, the person used is not necessarily bearing fruit, nor are the gifts a ticket to Heaven. When this reality sinks in, it will incite within God's soldiers that bearing fruit is vital for spiritual growth and should be our priority.

As his name declares, holiness characterizes the divine nature of the Holy Spirit. He endeavors to impart holiness to us and give us his divine nature and character. This is developed within us through the fruit of the Spirit. The more we decrease and allow him to increase in us, the more fruit is produced, and the more Christlike we become.

Let's look at the fruit for a better understanding of how it brings about a life that will walk in conquering power. In other words, enable us to be Christlike.

LOVE

> And we have known and believed the love that God hath to us. God is love; and he that dwelleth in love dwelleth in God, and God in him (1 John 4:16).

Because God is love, it is essential for love to dominate the virtues of our lives. This love refers to the selfless, God-kind of love that's more than willing to make personal sacrifices for the cause of Christ. It has no hidden agenda of self-gain, but is only concerned with the benefit of others.

> Though I speak with the tongues of men and of angels, and have not charity (love), I am become as sounding brass, or a tinkling cymbal. And though I have the gift of

prophecy, and understand all mysteries, and all knowledge; and though I have all faith, so that I could remove mountains, and have not charity (love), I am nothing. And though I bestow all my goods to feed the poor, and though I give my body to be burned, and have not charity (love), it profiteth me nothing (1 Corinthians 13:1-3).

The love which results from the fruit of the Spirit in our life is selfless and not selfish. It's a supernatural love operating through us. It's a fruit of the Spirit and cannot be self-produced. It's not the love of our self-efforts or for self-gain.

We who are Spirit-filled have to ask ourselves whether we are aiming simply for gifts, power, anointing, etc., or are we seeking the love that produces these things. If we dwell in love, it will bring the presence of God to every life situation.

The love of the Holy Spirit will never be self-centered. It's a love encouraging us to deny self, for it will place in us a desire to love God with all our heart, all our soul, all our mind, all our strength, and love our neighbor as our self (Mark 12:30-31).

JOY

For the kingdom of God is not meat and drink; but righteousness, and peace, and joy in the Holy Ghost (Romans 14:17).

The joy of the Holy Spirit is a strong inner sense of gladness not based on our circumstances. It is a joy which produces the character of Christ in us and can be an emotional response from a sense of well-being, tranquility, peacefulness, or exuberant gladness. Our joy can be expressed in singing, shouting, clapping, dancing, etc.

This joy is not emitted by our efforts. It's only produced by the Holy Spirit. True joy is not flesh activated by what we are experiencing in the natural. Just because we sing songs where we shout, clap, or dance, is not the joy of the Holy Spirit. It's trying to work up joy by our own methods.

We need to allow the character of God, who is true joy to become part of our character. Joy is part of God's nature. We become participants of his joy as we allow his nature to be developed in us.

Our joy is not dependent on our situations, our environment, people in our lives, or what we're going through at the time. Human happiness looks at the things in our life and is affected by our circumstances or what is going on around us. However, divine joy is unaffected by people, circumstances, or surrounding situations. Divine joy knows Heaven's benefits are unchanging.

It's a fact; our life can sometimes be painful, and we don't always have answers for what we are encountering. This is the time to look upward to God. True joy doesn't depend on our outer circumstances, but on our inner response to God during those difficult times.

PEACE

> Peace I leave with you, my peace I give unto you: not as the world giveth, give I unto you. Let not your heart be troubled, neither let it be afraid (John 14:27).

The peace of the Holy Spirit is the inner calm and contentment resulting from the knowledge that we are in a right relationship with God. It's knowing God has everything in control. The God who spoke all things into existence is able to control whatever may be in our lives. As He spoke peace to the storm (Luke 4:39), He's able to calm the storm within us.

As we allow the Holy Spirit to rule in our life, we have a soul-harmony that generates his peace. This divine peace is an experience so much profounder and more perpetual than happiness. This wonderful quality of love is an inner attribute expressing itself in peacefulness with God, with people, and with ourselves.

This divine peace is like being in the eye of a storm where there is calm. Yes, our life may be in a whirlwind, but our spirit is in the calm or peacefulness of God. Because we know Jesus is in the storm with us, we sleep on the pillow next to him.

LONGSUFFERING

> Take, my brethren, the prophets, who have spoken in the
> name of the Lord, for an example of suffering affliction,
> and of patience. Behold, we count them happy which en-
> dure. Ye have heard of the patience of Job, and have seen
> the end of the Lord; that the Lord is very pitiful, and of
> tender mercy (James 5:10-11).

Christlike character does not develop automatically or instantaneously, it requires diligence on our part to yield continually to the
Holy Spirit in every storm or obstacle we face in life. It's a constant
persevering in all our difficulties to yield to the Holy Spirit and not
to our flesh.

Longsuffering or patience is the ability to endure graciously
uncomfortable situations for an extended time. It's learning to be
content in whatever circumstance we may find ourselves (Philippians 4:11). For the Apostle Paul to pen such words meant he fully
understood difficult situations. He'd been beaten, stoned, suffered
shipwreck, in perils of water, in perils among false brethren, etc.
Yet, he endured because he knew he was in the will of God (2 Corinthians 11:23-33).

Patience is not an option for the Spirit-filled Christian, but an
essential virtue, it must be cultivated in our lives by surrendering
to the work of the Holy Spirit's power within us. It's not always easy
when we are waiting. Let's face it, many of God's soldiers have yet
to live in this virtue. However, it's during the waiting periods that
God could be preparing us for a task we may not yet be ready for.

Even when the situation appears to be hopeless, longsuffering
or patience doesn't give into despair. Longsuffering is endurance,
perseverance, and the ability to wait without becoming angry,
annoyed, or upset. It's also the capability to tolerate being hurt,
provoked, wrongly accused, etc. without losing our temper or
yielding to fleshly revenge. In short, it's a much-needed fruit or
characteristic to conquer this life.

GENTLENESS

> Now I Paul myself beseech you by the meekness and
> gentleness of Christ (2 Corinthians 10:1).

Gentleness is the word we use for kindness which is a perfect demonstration of Christ's love for treacherous sinners. As God showed such kindness to us who walked contrary to the will of God, Christ expects gentleness from us who claim to be his. If it's functioning in us, we will exhibit the same gentleness to others. However, gentleness is not concession. Jesus did not compromise his word in his gentleness toward us. Compromise is not gentleness but sedition against Christ.

Gentleness or kindness can be defined as caring, mercy, compassion, consideration, and concern for others. Cultivating gentleness involves a conscious effort to think of others before ourselves. True kindness is not something we demonstrate on holidays or special occasions. It should be a fundamental part of our Christian character displayed daily.

These acts of kindness can be as simple as a smile, a kind word, a listening ear, a word of encouragement, or simply being there when we are needed. Such kind acts can mean so much to others. This is especially true to those close to us, like our Christian husband or wife. Whenever we mistreat them, we are maltreating Christ who lives in them.

It's imperative that we encounter opportunities in our daily lives to show gentleness or kindness. Without the frequent exercise to show kindness to others, we'll unequivocally find ourselves back into our self-centered ways. When we are conscious of others, we become less conscious of self.

GOODNESS

> For the fruit of the Spirit is in all goodness and righteousness and truth (Ephesians 5:9).

True goodness is a quality of Christ's character in our hearts wrought by the Holy Spirit. It can be defined as the state of being righteous, generous, benevolent, etc. It's Godlikeness being expressed in what we do for others.

It's the goodness of God that generated our repentance (Romans 2:4). When we comprehended the love and goodness of God, it caused something in us to want to love him. We became aware of our sinful condition, repented, and asked him to save us. Likewise, as we yield to the Holy Spirit, He will enable us to reveal God's goodness in our dealings with the lost. In doing so, we may be the means whereby Christ is accepted as Savior.

FAITH

> Now faith is the substance of things hoped for, the evidence of things not seen. But without faith it is impossible to please him: for he that cometh to God must believe that he is, and that he is a rewarder of them that diligently seek him (Hebrews 11:1,6).

When it says that "now" faith is the substance, it means that at present, today, this present moment, this minute, etc. Faith is being sure and certain with complete confidence the God who promised will perform his promise. It's the present tense, not the future or past. We believe it right now whether or not it is seen. We hang onto our faith from the seedtime (time of the promise) until the harvest (fulfillment of the promise).

It's not based upon what we see in the natural. Faith takes God at his word and doesn't doubt his promises. We have confidence in God and not what the present circumstance may appear to be. We do not base our hope on the visible, but our confidence is in the spiritual reality.

In my books, *Faith's Journey Confronts Obstacles* and *Satan has no Authority Over God's Soldier*, I expound on what faith is. Faith originated in God and was here before the foundation of the world. God's faith spoke all things into existence, which means that He spoke the universe into existence out of nothing. Our faith is not in our ability, but in him who speaks, and things appear at his command (Isaiah 48:3). In other words, as God speaks, things that were not, all of a sudden appear. Once we realize this truth, we will never question God's ability to bring forth the promises He has given us.

MEEKNESS

Blessed are the meek: for they shall inherit the earth (Matthew 5:5).

Meekness does not indicate a weakness. In fact, a genuinely meek person will display great strength of character. It's a person who is patient, long-suffering, forbearing, etc. The meek are those who are not boisterous or selfishly aggressive, but are teachable. We understand we don't know it all, and we could be mistaken.

Jesus claimed to be meek in Matthew 11:29. It's clear that there was no weakness in him, for there was no greater strength or power displayed on earth by man. He fearlessly proclaimed the truth through all the difficulties He faced by the religious leaders plotting his death. He exercised power and authority over sin, devils, disease, death, and the elements of nature. His greatest strength was in his willingness to endure the agony of the cross. In doing so, He completed his earthly mission, utterly defeated Satan, and secured our redemption.

Meekness is acquired by yielding to the working of the Holy Spirit in our lives. As with all the fruit of the Spirit, it may manifest itself at times, but it will not be fully grown in us overnight. It must first blossom, then the small fruit appears, and as it is cultivated, it will grow, develop, and ripen.

TEMPERANCE

He that is slow to anger is better than the mighty; and he that ruleth his spirit than he that taketh a city (Proverbs 16:32).

Temperance is defined as self-control. It's the discipline of mastering our own desires, emotions, and passions. If we realize that we're the temple of the Holy Spirit, we will exercise control over our desires and motivations.

Temperance is having self-control over every aspect of our lives. It's control over anger, carnal passions, fleshly appetites, desire for worldly pleasures, self-centeredness, and the desire to be in control. Only as we yield to the Holy Spirit can his divine power overrule our carnal nature bent on the self-life.

As the Scripture reference reveals, if we rule our spirit, we are better than if we capture a city. As we nurture the fruit of temperance, our own appetites and desires will be submitted to the Holy Spirit and not allowed to rule us.

Our continuous self-denial and allowing the Spirit to have his way in our lives, will enable him to bring forth the fruit that will yield Christlikeness in us. We will have a strength of character that will be patient, longsuffering, and forbearing while walking in the power, authority, strength, and conquering power of the Holy Spirit.

Only as we submit to the lordship of Christ and are continually in submissive obedience to the Holy Spirit can the fruit of the Spirit be cultivated in us. This reminds me of a saying that I heard, *"where we tend a rose, a thistle cannot grow."* If we are mindful of nurturing our fruit, the works of the flesh cannot prosper.

Only as his fruit is developed, will we take on the Christlike character. Sin must be conquered, if we are to overcome this life, be clothed in white raiment, not have our name blotted out of the book of life, and have Jesus confess our name before his Father and his angels (Revelation 3:5). As we cultivate an intimate relationship with him and daily abide in Christ, we will become fruitful Christians who walk in the spirit and not the flesh. In doing so, his conquering power will be a reality in our life!

Chapter 8

Gifts of the Spirit

Now concerning spiritual gifts, brethren, I would not have you ignorant . . . Now there are diversities of gifts, but the same Spirit. And there are differences of administrations, but the same Lord. And there are diversities of operations, but it is the same God which worketh all in all. But the manifestation of the Spirit is given to every man to profit withal. For to one is given by the Spirit the word of wisdom; to another the word of knowledge by the same Spirit, To another faith by the same Spirit, to another the gifts of healing by the same Spirit, To another the working of miracles; to another prophecy, to another discerning of spirits, to another divers kinds of tongues; to another the interpretation of tongues.

—1 CORINTHIANS 12:1, 4-10

Before I expound upon this chapter, I felt it necessary to give a warning about the misunderstanding by many concerning the gifts of the Spirit. Young or immature Christians look at those using the gifts as if they are to be worshipped or something. Some have the erroneous belief that the gifts reveal the gifted are closer to God and are to be treated as superior to other Christians.

However, some of the gifted are living lives contrary to the righteousness and holiness expected by the Lord to inherit the kingdom of God. I will make it clearer as we go on in this chapter. But at present, I want to put up a red flag to warn God's soldiers that gifts **do not** equate spirituality, holiness, or a righteous life.

The apostle Paul was very concerned about the ignorance of spiritual gifts, and the negative effect on the church at Corinth. I believe common sense tells us, if the Spirit of God through Paul was concerned that the Corinthian Church shouldn't be ignorant about spiritual gifts, God is also concerned about today's church having a knowledge of the gifts.

In verse seven, Paul states the gifts are given to profit the whole church, not the individual in whom the gift is manifested. God doesn't give the gifts to us to be puffed up at how great we are because we flow in them. They are not for self-profit, but the benefit of all. In fact, if the gifts are not used in love (according to 2 Corinthians 13), the individual is nothing more than an irritating NOISE.

> For the promise is unto you, and to your children, and to all that are afar off, even as many as the Lord our God shall call (Acts 2:39).

There are many who question whether the Holy Spirit baptism was just to start the church age. However, Peter made clear in the above Scripture that it's to continue as long as men are being called to repentance. The promise of the Spirit and the call to salvation are the same today as when Peter spoke those words.

I do believe much of the confusion is due to all the misuse of the gifts and things being stated in the Name of the Lord, when the Holy Spirit wasn't in their prophesying. However, let me ask some questions to reveal how ridiculous Satan can get Christians to be.

If we buy a bag of potatoes and there are a couple of rotten ones in it, should we throw the whole bag away? If our milk goes sour, do we quit buying milk? Of course not, we would pick over the potatoes and keep the good ones. Also, we would throw the milk away or use it to make sourdough and buy another gallon.

What we have to understand is the devil knows the Holy Spirit baptism helps Christians to interpret or see the word as never before. It empowers us to live supernatural lives in this natural world. We're armed and dangerous to the enemy. However, with anything concerning human activity, the devil has deceived man to corrupt the gifts through fleshly measures.

Without the gifts of the Spirit operating in today's church, it becomes something quite different from what God intended. Instead of being the supernatural organism designed by God (functioning with the gifts), the church becomes merely a human organization void of any supernatural manifestations. It's powerless and death is breeding where life should be manifesting.

When the Holy Spirit baptism is not believed, there are no gifts operating. Thus, if the devil can deceive us into not wanting or not believing the baptism in the Spirit is for today or that we receive the baptism at conversion, there are no gifts to profit or edify the church. In spite of the misuse, they're much needed for spiritual power in the church.

Now, let's inspect the gifts and understand what would be missing in the church without them. To properly do this, we must divide them into three groups.

1. Gifts of utterance are the gifts that say something.
   a. Divers kinds of tongues.
   b. Interpretation of tongues.
   c. Prophecy.

2. Gifts of revelation are the gifts that reveal something.
   a. Word of wisdom.
   b. Word of knowledge.
   c. Discerning of spirits.

3. Gifts of power are the gifts that do something.

a.   Gift of faith.
b.   Working of miracles.
c.   Gifts of healings.

GIFTS OF UTTERANCE

The gifts of utterance say or express something aloud. The Holy Spirit communicates to the church through the use of these gifts. As all the gifts, they are supernatural manifestations of the Spirit and not natural manifestations of the person.

Divers kinds of tongues

Divers kinds of tongues is a supernatural utterance by the Holy Spirit. It's a language never learned by the speaker and not understood in the mind of the speaker. This language cannot be learned, it's supernatural through the Spirit.

I want to make something clear; this language is not the person's individual prayer language which is the evidence of being baptized in the Spirit. Let's understand, it's not supernatural in the sense that the Holy Spirit takes control of us and forces us to speak. In fact, it has nothing to do with our linguistic ability.

When we speak in tongues, we release our tongue, our vocal chords to the indwelling Holy Spirit who then gives the supernatural manifestation. It can be somewhat frightening to us at first to find ourselves speaking in an unknown language and hearing something coming through our vocal chords that we have no idea of what's being said. However, this is where faith comes in. It can be explained as walking on the water.

As a matter of fact, it's really quite an exciting experience as the Holy Spirit moves upon us. When He prompts us in the gift of divers kinds of tongues to speak out in the congregation, He bubbles up inside, our heart seems to beat faster with the expectation. Then as we yield our tongue and vocal chords, He brings forth the unknown language.

Interpretation of tongues

Interpretation of tongues is the gift needed to interpret the gift of tongues. It's a supernatural gift bringing forth what is said in tongues. This is not a translation. It's an interpretation. A translation is a word for word utterance. An interpretation brings forth the meaning of the tongues.

With the interpretation of tongues there is also a prompting. When the Holy Spirit comes upon us to interpret, the first couple of words will come to our mind. As we speak them, He gives us more. It's sort of like someone dictating. As we write what is said down, more is dictated until finished.

Tongues without interpretation in the church are meaningless and out of order (1 Corinthians 14:5-13). Thus, the speaker in tongues is dependent upon the interpreter for the completion of his message. If we also have the gift of interpretation, the Holy Spirit will give us the interpretation to what we just spoke in tongues.

The interpretation of tongues is a supernatural gift and is entirely dependent upon the gift of divers kinds of tongues and has no function apart from that gift. Unless, we also have the gift of interpretation or are aware that another Christian has the gift of interpretation, we do not speak out. This gift is the ability to interpret the message given in tongues in a language understood by the hearers.

Prophecy

The gift of prophecy is a supernatural speech in a known language. It's the voice of the Holy Spirit using our vocal chords. This gift should not be confused with the prophetic office. It's one of the utterance gifts and doesn't make us a prophet.

Prophecy means to speak for another. It's speaking one's own language in the power of the Holy Spirit. In the Old Testament it was essentially foretelling (futuristic), whereas, in the New Testament it is forth-telling (unfolding the word).

To constitute the office of a Prophet, we would have to have the same gifts as the Old Testament Prophets. As such, we would possess at least two of the revelation gifts plus the gift of prophesy. In other words, we have the gift of the word of wisdom and or the gift of the word of knowledge and or the gift of discerning of spirits as well as prophecy.

Prophecy is the only gift that we are told to covet (1 Corinthians 14:1,3). We can all prophecy, but we cannot all be Prophets. Some are trying to foretell instead of forth-tell and are opening themselves up to wrong spirits. The more we try to manifest a gift in a way it's not meant to be used, we're walking on dangerous ground and giving place to seducing spirits.

The gift of prophecy operates only when there's a special unction placed upon us by the Holy Spirit to deliver a specific message of Divine inspiration. In a general sense, it refers to proclaiming and thus to preaching.

Technically, a Prophet was not only able to proclaim God's message, but was able to predict the future. All the Prophet's messages whether proclaiming or predicting came from God directly through special revelation.

Prophecy is to be for:

1. **Edification** (1 Corinthians 14:3, 4, 31). This is to strengthen the saints, to increase their faith, and to develop their Christian character. It's not meant to be used to tear down maliciously through the guise of the gift of prophecy.

2. **Exhortation** is such a distinctive phase of the gift of prophecy that it's dignified by being called a gift itself (Romans 12:8).

   It's also misunderstood by many in this phase when it's used to turn us from wrong to right, from error to truth, from unbelief to obedience and faith. Some have claimed that it is tearing down. However, it's the Holy Spirit *warning* of the consequences of sin and the need of repentance.

   God loves and God pleads through the gift of prophecy.

3. **Comfort.** One of the Holy Spirit's major names is Comforter (John 14:26). It is He who comforts us (1 Corinthians 14:31).

Let me interject something here that's vital. These ministers using personal prophecy to enhance their ministry or through their own pride to be needed by the people have ruined many lives. Many unfortunate things have happened through misuse.

I want to make clear that a direct prophecy to us as an individual should always be a **conformation** of what God has already placed in our heart or confirmed in at least one other clear and definite way.

To help clarify misuse of the gift of prophecy, I will tell a personal story. When I was a young Christian, I attended a Bible study. After the study, certain ones were going around giving personal prophecies. I had this wrong feeling inside. It was strong, but being too unlearned in the Scriptures, I didn't know what it was.

Anyway, I felt the Holy Spirit impress me to leave and to not go back. After several weeks, I learned the Pastor of the Church heard about the Bible study, the things going on, and shut it down. He had gone to visit without giving anyone any impression of what he had heard was transpiring. After the study, when all the so-called personal prophecies began to be given to different individuals, he rebuked the error. They were yielding to wrong spirits. He informed all attending that it was not of God.

Personal prophecy through misuse has ruined many lives and many unfortunate things have happened through its abuse. Individuals have been directed through so-called prophecy to sell their homes, sell their business, quit their job, and more. Sadly, more often than not, the advice was not of God.

I want to reiterate that if anyone gives us a direct prophecy, it will always be a confirmation to what God has already been laying on our heart. It will not be something God has not revealed to us. In other words, it will not be something that we have not sensed, etc. It will be confirmation of what God has been revealing. It will never contradict the word of God. Furthermore, the gift of prophecy does not make us a Prophet. That must be fully understood. While we are to covet the gift of prophecy, the gift will not make us a Prophet.

GIFTS OF REVELATION

Before we start the revelation gifts, I want to make clear that we cannot be a recipient used in these gifts or manifestation until we are baptized in the Holy Spirit.

Many believers who are not baptized in the Spirit will tell us God has used them in these gifts (except tongues and interpretation). This is not possible. They are confused with what is natural to the born-again life and what the gifts really are.

Now, I want to make emphatically clear that although the gifts are given to us, the gift is not controlled (turned on and off) by us. We don't control the gift. It's the discretion of the Holy Spirit when and where the gift is to manifest. The gifts are the manifestations of the Holy Spirit, but not for personal edification. If a gift is turned on by the person, it's not the gift of the Holy Spirit.

Let me explain what I mean. When Moses was doing his miracles, the wise men and sorcerers of Pharaoh did likewise (Exodus 7:11). Not all things are of God, and not all claiming to be a Christian belong to Christ.

As I stated, the gifts are not for personal edification. My prayer language is the result of the Holy Spirit baptism. It's the evidence that I have received the Spirit's baptism (Acts 2:4). My prayer language belongs to me, and whenever I yield to the Holy Spirit, my prayer language comes forth. It's not my using my gift of divers kinds of tongues, it's my personal prayer language. 1 Corinthians 14:4 says: he that prays in an unknown tongue (personal prayer language, not the gift of divers kinds of tongues) **edifieth** himself. That tongue (my prayer language) is for my personal edification to build me up in the faith.

According 1 Corinthians 12:7, the gift of tongues is to edify the whole body. The gifts of the Spirit are given to the body to profit everyone. Furthermore, the ministerial gifts of apostles, prophets, evangelists, pastors, teachers are for the perfecting of the saints, for the work of the ministry, and for the edifying of the body of Christ (Ephesians 4:8, 11-12). As the ministers are gifts to the church, so are the gifts of the Spirit. They are meant to edify the body and not for self-exaltation.

Although we will look at these gifts individually, they often operate with other gifts as I will bring out further on in this chapter. Now let's look at the revelation gifts.

Word of wisdom

> If any of you lack wisdom, let him ask of God, that giveth to all men liberally, and upbraideth not; and it shall be given him (James 1:5).

Let's comprehend that possessing wisdom is not the gift. Wisdom is something we need in our day to day lives. God promises to give wisdom liberally, abundantly, freely, generously to all who ask.

However, the gift of the word of wisdom is given to one by the Holy Spirit at his discretion. It's not because we asked for it. We cannot ask for any of the gifts. This truth must be comprehended.

Please understand the word of wisdom is just that "a word." It's not the gift of wisdom, but a word. A word is just a fragmentary part of the whole. God is all wise and all knowing, but He only reveals a part of it to us. It's what He wants us to know.

The word of wisdom always speaks of the future; it never speaks of the past or present. It is things in the mind of God pertaining to the yet to come. Earlier, I explained the difference between the gift of prophecy and the prophetic office. The gift of prophecy does not constitute the office of a prophet.

As the Old Testament prophet used prophecy along with the gift of the word of wisdom, word of knowledge, or discerning of spirits, so will the New Testament prophet. What this is saying is that a true prophet today can give a word of wisdom or a word of knowledge through prophecy.

Let me interject at this point a truth about being called to the ministry. Please understand just because we have the gift of the word of wisdom, doesn't make us a prophet. Neither does a word of wisdom being used mean we prophesied. Too many are confused about the ministerial gifts and believe because of a certain gift or talent makes them an apostle, prophet, etc.

It's imperative to realize if we are born again, we can be called to the five-fold ministry by Christ. He will make his calling quite clear. Don't get me wrong, I do believe there are apostles and prophets today. However, it seems like they are crawling out of the woodwork. Pride has multitudes claiming to be Apostle So and So or Prophet So and So to enhance their self-called or man-called ministry.

As the multitude in the Old Testament were false prophets, it's a sad truth today. We're over run with self-called or man-called apostles and prophets. What I mean by this, is as we know we have had encounter with Jesus Christ and are born-again. We know Jesus called us to the ministry. As we can vividly remember our salvation experience, we can vividly remember when He called us.

A laying on of hands for ordination is to confirm God's call on our life. It's not man claiming we are called, when Christ never personally called us. Salvation is a personal experience and so is a call to ministry.

Okay, lets' get on with the gift of the word of wisdom. It can be given by an audible voice, a vision, or through a dream. When Joseph had his dreams of his brethren bowing down to him, it was a word of wisdom revealing future happenings.

Any time revelation gifts are used, it's always a word of wisdom (future happenings), a word of knowledge (past or present happenings), or the discerning of spirits.

Now, just because a word of wisdom is given does not mean the individual knows all the circumstances to come about, but only what God has revealed. I know this to be true. Do you think if I had known the woman in my church was going to be murdered that I would not have warned her more adamantly?

The only word God gave me was that her son was not to start school his senior year in the town they were living in. When I went to her and asked if God had been dealing with them to move before her son started his senior year. She said He had, but she had taken it up with God and it was settled; her son would finish school and then they would move.

I told her I was confused. If everything is fine with God, why has He sent me to you three times. She told me it was between me and God. But as far as she was concerned, she and God had it all worked out. Of course, in my previous book, *Satan Has no Authority Over God's Soldier: Illuminating Godlike Faith*, I revealed she was brutally murdered the day her son started his senior year.

That was a word of wisdom. I didn't know all the details. God had made it clear her son was not to start his senior year in the town. This was referring to the future.

Word of knowledge

Gift of word of knowledge has nothing to do with things we can learn or already know through our education. It's a supernatural revelation of information pertaining to people, places, things, or events in the mind of God referring to the past or present. It's never future.

This gift can also come through a vision, a dream, or prophesy. When Jesus dealt with the Canaan woman at the well, He used this gift. He told her what she did in the past and what she was presently doing.

When the Lord had me prophesy at our wedding, He used the gift of the word of wisdom and the word of knowledge. God went back to the Garden when He created Adam and Eve and explained what marriage was all about (word of knowledge of the past). Then He said these two are mine (word of knowledge of the present). He ended with stating that He would send us forth to do his work (word of wisdom of the future).

Discerning of spirits

Discerning of spirits is not what Hebrews 5:13-14 is referring to. Those verses teach as we mature, are off the milk of the word as babes, and become skillful in the word, we are endowed by the Holy Spirit to discern both good and evil. Likewise, 1 John 4:1-3 is not the gift. It's the Holy Spirit leading us to try the spirits to see if they are of God, because many false prophets are out there proclaiming what is not of God or his word. It's a gospel that appeals to the flesh or the old nature. The spirit of antichrist is rampant, and we must become proficient in the word to recognize these contrary spirits.

The gift of discerning of spirits doesn't come through being proficient in the word, it's given at the moment needed. As all the gifts, it's bestowed when the Holy Spirit sees the need for it to manifest. It pertains to the spirit world which includes evil spirits, Divine spirits, and human spirits.

1. **Evil spirits** are demons, fallen angels, Satan.

2. **Divine spirits** are hosts of Heaven: angels, cherubim, seraphim, the Lord.

3. **Human spirits** are of man who is a tripartite being of spirit, soul, body.

This gift of spiritually discerning spirits is the ability to distinguish between the word and the false doctrines of devils. Yes, we are all able to discern as we mature in the word. But when the gift manifests, it's a sudden recognition that what is being taught is deception transmitted by demonic spirits through human spirits.

Let me give an example of this gift in operation. My husband and I were at this Bible study. The person was teaching that when Jesus said to deny self, He didn't mean to sacrifice comforts and pleasures. Jesus came to give us an abundant life and too many are using self asceticism thinking they are holy.

The Holy Spirit immediately quickened me that this was the voice of the antichrist spirit, and I told my husband who was looking at me with a puzzled look. We just got up and left. Some that we knew, followed us out. They and my husband said they didn't get the right feeling about what he was teaching. I told them it was the antichrist spirit. Anyway, they were using their natural ability to discern both good and evil. Whereas, the gift manifested in me and named the spirit.

Let me explain something here, it's not the gift of discerning of spirits to know when someone is a false teacher or giving false doctrine. Because the Spirit of God will make it known to us; we don't need man to teach us about seducing spirits (1 John 2:25–27).

I mentioned earlier that when I was a young Christian, I attended a Bible study. There were different individuals giving personal prophecies. It was strong in me that something was wrong. The Holy Spirit impressed me to leave and to not go back. Later on, I learned the Pastor of the church closed it down.

Now, I wasn't using the gift of discerning of spirits, the Holy Spirit was prompting me that what was coming forth was not of God. The ability to discern what is truth or lie is what the Holy Spirit does. It's He who guides us into all truth (John 16:13). All Christians who yield to the Spirit will have such discerning ability. As we mature, we'll be able to back up what we sense by Scripture.

Let me interject a thought here. I have heard many claim to have the gift of discernment. However, there's no such gift. Discernment is simply being guided by the Holy Spirt into truth to discern what is good or evil. Furthermore, it's the gift of discerning of spirits.

This gift is more limited than the word of wisdom and the word of knowledge because its range is limited to only spirits. Whereas, the other two deal with a broader scope applying to people, places, things, and events.

The gift of discerning of spirits is not psychological insight. It's not mental penetration. It's not the power to discern the faults of others. The knack to discern faults is possessed by believers and unbelievers. We don't have to be born-again to get the "gift" of suspicion of others.

Now, I'm not saying the gift of discerning of spirits is needed to sense the powers of Hell at work. The Holy Spirit will reveal that to us, as I stated about the Bible study I attended as a young Christian. All Christians who yield to the Holy Spirit will discern what is good or evil (what is of God and what is not of God). However, there are times that those who have the gift will suddenly recognize what spirit it is. It's perhaps a less used gift, nevertheless, it's used when the Holy Spirit sees fit.

GIFTS OF POWER

Before I discuss these gifts, it must be understood that these gifts are supernatural and not natural. Furthermore, I want to reiterate that the gifts of the Spirit sometimes work in conjunction with each other.

When it appears that one is in operation, it may be two or three actually at work.

Gift of Faith

Gift of faith is not talking about the faith that all believers possess.

> Now faith is the substance of things hoped for, the evidence of things not seen (Hebrews 11:1).

So many in the church seem to be seeking faith, when in reality, few really understand what faith is.

Many things can be said about faith. Faith is a present-tense matter, because it's a present-tense activity. Whereas, hope is future tense.

Faith is believing before seeing the fulfillment. Faith eventually brings into reality what a person starts out by believing. Faith is not passive, it is active.

It must be understood that the gift of faith is different from the faith which is a fruit of the Spirit. Scripture makes clear that God has given us all the measure faith (Romans 12:3). We all have the measure of faith given to us at conversion. This is not the gift of faith.

So many think if I had the gift of faith, I could believe this or that. The faith to believe God is already in us. All we have to do is use it. As a body builder builds up his muscles through exercise, faith is built up through exercise. This is explained in my book, *Storms Are Faith's Workout: Preparing Christians for Spiritual Ambush.*

Please understand the gift of faith is not like the faith we receive as a fruit of the Spirit, which takes time to strengthen. With the gift of faith, it happens instantaneously. When this occurs, there is a sudden surge of faith or special faith that's supernatural and miraculous.

It usually happens in a crisis situation or an extreme predicament. Suddenly there is a great confidence and belief, usually coupled with the irresistible urge to declare something in the Name of Jesus with the absolute certainty it will come to pass.

Hear me, there must be a specific need in order for the Holy Spirit to activate this gift. We will not receive the gift of faith by simply desiring or requesting it.

I will reveal in the working of miracles how the gift of faith works in synergy with the other gifts.

Working of Miracles

Working of miracles is seen in Joshua 10:12-14 where the sun stood still until the battle was won. In 2 Kings 20:8-11 shows the sundial being put back ten degrees. Matthew 14:25-33 reveals Jesus walked on the water. Mark 4:39-40 shows Jesus causing the storm to cease.

We use the word miracle so generally today that many don't even know what a miracle actually is. A miracle is a supernatural intervention in the ordinary course of nature. An interruption of the system of nature, as we know it, operated by the force of the Spirit of God, as seen in the verses listed above.

The biggest danger is when Christians start to flock to the supernatural events and to follow miracles rather than following Jesus. We must all be cautious of the "miracle syndrome" especially as more and more people experiment with the occult and psychic powers.

In my book, *Faith's Journey Confronts Obstacles: Instructing God's Soldiers to Overcome in His Armor*, I give an example on page fifty-seven of the gift of faith and the working of miracles. It doesn't state which gifts were involved, because that wasn't the intention of the book. I will not repeat the episode here. However, I will state that a three-story building was lifted up by the power of God.

Gifts of Healing

Gifts of healing is not the laying on of hands on the sick and them recovering according to James 5:14-15. Again, I must reiterate the gifts are sudden and given at the moment. It's not something we can pray up to or turn on at will. They are supernatural occurrences by the Holy Spirit.

When the gifts of healing is in operation, we are healed instantly of whatever infirmity or disease. This is a supernatural cure. It has no explanation for it, except that it's done, and we're supernaturally healed. Simply put, it is miraculous.

It's necessary to understand the gifts are not controlled by the individual with the gifts. The Holy Spirit decides when and where a specific gift is to function. We have no control over them. I want to make this clear, because I've had people ask why those with the gifts of healing don't go and empty out all the hospitals.

Let me explain that Jesus was at the Pool of Bethesda where a great multitude of sick people, blind, lame, paralyzed waited for the moving of the water. Now, Jesus only healed the man who had suffered from his infirmity for thirty-eight years (John 5: 1-8).

All who are born again have the potential for the fruit of the Spirit to be blossoming in our life. However, the gifts are given to whosoever the Spirit wills. The fruit is to help us live a holy, faith filled, overcoming life. They are to benefit us personally, whereas, the gifts are meant to benefit or profit the whole body of Christ. They are not to puff-up the recipient of the gift. Neither are those who don't possess the gifts to look at those with them as if they are highly favored by God. That's why it's imperative to see if the tree is bearing fruit or is it fruitless. Examine the personal life of anyone who uses the gifts before accepting that they represent the God of the Bible.

The devil uses many to reproduce gifts and lead many astray. This is why so many will believe the lying signs and wonders of the anti-Christ. However, all of us have the ability through the Holy Spirit to discern whether it's of God or not.

What I am trying to convey is that we don't throw out the baby with the bath water. The gifts are a vital component to the church. Without the gifts of the Spirit in today's church, the body of Christ becomes merely a human organization. Whereas, God designed the church to be a supernatural organism. Without the functioning of the gifts, the church becomes powerless!

Chapter 9

Baptism of Fire

For our God is a consuming fire.

—HEBREWS 12:29

I indeed baptize you with water unto repentance: but he that cometh after me is mightier than I, who shoes I am not worthy to bear: he shall baptize you with the Holy Ghost and with fire.

—MATTHEW 3:11

Whose fan is in his hand, and he will thoroughly purge his floor, and will gather the wheat into his garner; but the chaff he will burn with fire unquenchable.

—LUKE 3:17

This chapter will reveal why so many of God's soldiers are not living in conquering power, and yet, we have been baptized in the Holy Spirit. Most of us have the mentality that the baptism in the Spirit is to fill us with supernatural power. While that is true, we forget about the fire.

We seek after the gifts to promote us or our ministry and not the Lord. It's imperative to realize the gifts are to profit the whole body of Christ (1 Corinthians 12:7). If we are not purified, we'll covet the best gifts to profit self. This is why we must allow the Holy Spirit to do his cleansing work by fire.

> And he shall sit as a refiner and purifier of silver: and he shall purify the sons of Levi, and purge them as gold and silver, that they may offer unto the LORD an offering in righteousness (Malachi 3:3).

We need to comprehend that we are to be holy as He is holy (1 Peter 1:16). As we picture a refiner sitting by his fire to purify gold or silver, this is what God is doing to us through the baptism of fire.

The baptism in the Holy Spirit is going to first be a cleansing fire to purify what needs to be eliminated from our life. This is how the Spirit does his reconstructing work in us. If we're to walk in conquering power, we have to be purified of all the dross inhibiting the Spirit from having his way in our life. Sin of any kind will interfere with the working of the conquering power in our life.

Because we have a free will, He will not purge us against our will. If we desire to hang onto what He wants gone, He will not take it. We must, of our own free will, desire to let it go. In other words, we have to hate the sin and want it out of our life.

> Not everyone that saith unto me, Lord, Lord, shall enter into the kingdom of heaven; but he that doeth the will of my Father which is in heaven. Many will say to me in that day, Lord, Lord, have we not prophesied in thy name? and in thy name have cast out devils? and in thy name done many wonderful works? And then will I profess unto them, I never knew you: depart from me, ye that work iniquity (Matthew 7:21-23).

In the above scriptures, Jesus makes clear that *not* everyone calling him Lord will enter into the kingdom of heaven. Only those who do the will of the Father in heaven. If we're not doing God's purposes and requirements, we're not executing his will in our life. This is not teaching that we can earn our salvation, for it is a gift of God (Ephesians 2:8-9). However, obedience to his will is a result and the outcome of salvation that conquers this world. We need to comprehend salvation is something to revere. Otherwise, we will trod under our feet the Son of God and count his blood of the covenant as unholy and do despite the Spirit of grace (Hebrews 10:29). How many are selling their birthright (salvation) for a morsel of meat (fleshly appetites) as Esau?

Too many think moving in the gifts elevate them in God's eyes, and continue in the sins that will not inherit the kingdom of God. Jesus makes clear obedience to God's will is a continuous prerequisite for salvation. We are to deny self and not allow sin to reign in our mortal bodies (Luke 9:23; Romans 6:12).

Listen to me, we need to stop looking at someone's huge ministry, their gifts, their supernatural power to cast out demons, etc. We need to observe their personal life. What is it reflecting? Is it done for personal gain? Do they think they deserve to be wealthy and live in luxury while those under them are poor? Do they love the accolades and worship of people? Do they put themselves on a pedestal? In simple terms, do they love Jesus or self? Their life will reveal the truth to those who discern truth.

This is not judging. It's making righteous judgment encouraged by Christ (John 7:24). He further made clear that we will know a tree by its fruit (Luke 6:43–45).

Christian, instead of listening and following those with huge ministries, start being a fruit inspector. What is their personal life reflecting? Is it the flesh or the fruit of the Spirit? Are they more concerned with quantity and not quality? In other words, are they endeavoring to make disciples of Christ or disciples of themselves?

A person truly yielding to the Holy Spirit's fire will be more concerned about fruit in their life and not how many gifts they have. Not that we don't know what our gifts are, but we realize without obedience to God's will, we could risk hearing Jesus never knew us.

> When I shall say to the righteous, that he shall surely live: if he trust to his own righteousness, and commit iniquity, all his righteousness shall **not be remembered**; but for his iniquity that he hath committed, he shall die for it. Again, when I say unto the wicked, Thou shalt surely die; if he turn from his sin, and do that which is lawful and right; If the wicked restore the pledge, give again that he had robbed, walk in the statutes of life, without committing iniquity; he shall surely live, he shall not die. **None of his sins** that he hath committed **shall be mentioned unto him:** he hath done that which is lawful and right; he shall surely live (Ezekiel 33: 13-16).

The verses in Ezekiel clarify the scriptures in Matthew. I had sought the Lord as to how He could claim to not know someone who had been doing great works for him. He quickened me to Ezekiel and its truth. If we turn from our righteousness and commit sin without repenting, all our previous righteousness will not be remembered. This means we stopped doing the will of God and turned to do our own will. If we die in an unrepentant state of sin, we will not inherit the kingdom of God. Too many believe false teachings saying they can remain in sin of any kind and are going to Heaven because they said a sinner's prayer.

Yes, Jesus died on the cross to give forgiveness for our past, present, and future sins. This doesn't mean we come to Jesus and continue to live in sin and are forgiven. It means through repentance, we will be forgiven for past sins, present sins, and future sins. We are only forgiven as we repent and turn from the sin. Repentance is a one-hundred-eighty degree turn. We are not forgiven if we do not repent.

Make no mistake about that truth. If more information about the deceitfulness of sin is needed, my book *Spiritual Shipwreck on the Horizon: Exhorting Christians to Contend for the Faith and Comprehend the Deceitfulness of Sin* will illuminate how so many are deceived and living in sins the Bible clearly states will not inherit the kingdom of God.

Jesus states in Matthew chapter 7, that many who are believing they are serving God and are moving in the gifts are not going to Heaven. They have turned from their righteousness unto unrighteousness. All they did prior to their deviating from God's will is no longer remembered.

We cannot expect to live in the sins that will not inherit the kingdom of God and believe we are in a right relationship with God and heading to Heaven. It's of the utmost importance to understand that conquering power is the result of doing the Father's will, denying self, and refusing to allow sin in our life. Jesus proved this truth by his life and his death.

If the Holy Spirit's fire is doing his work in us, we will more and more be living a Christlike life. It will be him increasing and us decreasing. The hotter the fire, the purer our life becomes as sin's rule is broken through repentance. As this happens, we will walk more and more in conquering power. That power comes through the baptism of the cleansing fire!

Chapter 10

The Resurrected Soldier

What shall we say then? Shall we continue in sin, that grace may abound? God forbid. How shall we, that are dead to sin, live any longer therein? Know ye not, that so many of us as were baptized into Jesus Christ were baptized into his death? Therefore we are buried with him by baptism into death: that like as Christ was raised up from the dead by the glory of the Father, even so we also should walk in newness of life. For if we have been planted together in the likeness of his death, we shall be also in the likeness of his resurrection: Knowing this, that our old man is crucified with him, that the body of sin might be destroyed, that henceforth we should not serve sin. For he that is dead is freed from sin. Now if we be dead with Christ, we believe that we shall also live with him: Knowing

that Christ being raised from the dead dieth
no more; death hath no more dominion over
him. For in that he died, he died unto sin
once: but in that he liveth, he liveth unto God.
Likewise reckon ye also yourselves to be dead
indeed unto sin, but alive unto God through
Jesus Christ our Lord. Let not sin therefore
reign in your mortal body, that ye should
obey it in the lusts thereof. Neither yield ye
your members as instruments of unrighteousness unto sin: but yield yourselves unto God,
as those that are alive from the dead, and
your members as instruments of righteousness
unto God.

—ROMANS 6:1-13

In this chapter, we need to think of resurrection in a different way. As God's soldiers, we always think of Christ's resurrection and our future resurrection from the dead. However, in this chapter, we need to perceive resurrection as the daily course of our life. It's the foundation on which we live our lives as Christians. It's the process by which we are reconstructed daily into the new creation in Christ.

What is the definition of the word resurrection? According to the Oxford Dictionary of current English, it is defined as: rising from the dead; Christ's rising from the dead; **Revival** after disease, inactivity, or decay.

When I pondered those definitions, I believe the Lord wants us to comprehend for this chapter, it's revival after decay and the rising from the dead.

As we set the foundation, we need to keep in mind "revival after decay" and "rising from the dead." At the same time, we must remember we are talking about the resurrected soldier.

Before we look at our Scripture text in Romans, we need to see what occurred before these verses. Paul proved salvation to both the Jew and Gentile must come through the Messiah. This salvation is received by faith only. Now, in this chapter, he reveals Christians have an obligation to live a holy life and the advantages of living such a life.

God's soldiers must understand God requires two principles of us. First, we are to have a holy heart, and secondly, we are to live a holy life. This is why the baptism of fire must be allowed to have its way in our life. Because we are to live a holy life, the apostle Paul asks if we should continue in sin that grace may abound.

Let me explain, there are some who think that because salvation is simply believing in Jesus Christ and his finished work on the cross, and because Jesus took our sins upon himself, that sin can do him or her no harm. Many believe they now have favor with God and sin no longer matters.

Paul goes on to claim that sin should not be part of our life. How can we who are dead to sin live any longer in it? This is a serious question and one that must not be taken lightly.

Listen to me, if we die to something or someone, it means we are totally separated from them. In other words, we can no longer have contact with them, and he/she can no longer have contact with us.

If we live to something or someone, we are to be wholly given up to them. Our whole being is theirs. To us, as Christians to live for Christ means we have no life; for our life is his. Everything belongs to him. He is master. He is Lord, He is everything. He is our very life.

Next, Paul talks about baptism in water. This is the first step of obedience on our faith walk. It's when we publicly proclaim Christ is our Lord and Savior. When we are water baptized, it's an outer profession of our receiving the doctrine of Christ crucified. Thus, it's proof of the genuineness of our faith.

However, it means that we now have an obligation to live according to its precepts. It's one thing to say we believe in the doctrine of Christ, but it's another to live it. Remember, a tree is known by its fruit. Our fruit (our life) is what shows whether we believe what our mouth says.

The words baptized into his death is the key to this chapter. When Jesus died on the cross, he died completely. There was no spark of the natural life remaining in his body. His fleshly body was lifeless.

Now, it says that we are buried with him by baptism into his death. What does this mean? It means exactly what it says. If Jesus died on the cross and the natural life was gone, He was dead to his flesh. This is saying that when we were baptized or immersed into water, something was dead. As Christ was dead to his flesh, we are proclaiming that we have died to our flesh.

We all know about planting. When the seed or plant is inserted into the ground, it derives from the ground all its nourishment. It obtains all the nutrients allowing it to grow and get firm, strong, and vigorous until it puts forth its blossoms and fruit from the earth that it has been planted into.

It's like when Jesus said He was the vine and we are the branches (John 15:5). The branches receive all their strength from the vine. Well, it was Christ's death on the cross that gave him the strength, so to speak, to redeem mankind. Without the death on the cross, man would be eternally lost in sin.

Through his vicarious death, we derive the pardon and holiness that is our salvation from the punishment due us for our sins. Whether we understand it or not, we still deserve to go to Hell. It's only as we continue in the faith and holiness required that we will conquer this life and miss Hell. Our salvation is not complete until we overcome this life. Only those who **overcome** will inherit all things (Revelation 21:7).

Christ's sacrificial death is the soil in which Christians are planted, and from which we derive our life, fruitfulness, and our final glory. When it states that our old man is crucified with him, it is saying our old man is that seed planted. It represents the death of the whole body. We go under the water to symbolize our death to self and come up out of the water to symbolize our new life in Christ.

Let's explain planting of a seed a little further. All seeds are composed of two parts. First is the germ which contains the rudiments of the future plant. Second is the lobes or body of the seed, which by their decomposition in the ground or their decaying in the ground, becomes the first nourishment to the extremely fine and delicate roots of the embryo plant, and support it until it is capable of deriving more nourishment from the soil.

The body dies so the germ may live. Jesus said in John 12:24: except a corn of wheat fall into the ground and die, it abideth alone: but if it die, it bringeth forth much fruit. In other words, it brings forth new life. The old life (the seed) is decayed so that the new life can burst forth.

How is this principle of new life which Jesus Christ has implanted in us to be brought into full effect and usefulness? It's through the destruction of the body of sin, our old man, our wicked, corrupt, and fleshly self. If we are to walk in the Holy Spirit's conquering power over the devil, self, sin, sickness, etc., our carnal nature, that desires to sin, must be crucified.

We must die to self as Christ was crucified, that our souls may be raised from a death of sin to a life of righteousness. Water baptism symbolizes that as the body of Christ was raised from the grave, so is our old man crucified and the new man raised from the dead.

The body of Christ died that He may be a quickening Spirit to mankind. In order to have new life, something must die. In plants, it is the seed. Well, in Christians, it is the body of sin. Not our physical body, but the old man or the sinful nature. This means we are supposed to be dead to carnality, our sinful nature, the old man with its lusts of the flesh, lusts of the eyes, and the pride of life.

Christ died unto sin once. This means He died on account of our sin once. He doesn't have to die to sin again. Likewise reckon ye also yourselves to be dead indeed unto sin, but alive unto God through Jesus Christ our Lord. We are to die as truly to sin as Christ died for sin, and we are to live truly unto God as Christ lives with God.

No, we are not dead in the physical sense. It's a reckoning that our old man, the sinful nature is dead. If we consider our old man dead, then we have been freed from the power sin.

> Jesus answered them, Verily, verily, I say unto you, Whosoever committeth sin is the servant of sin. And the servant abideth not in the house forever: but the Son abideth ever. If the Son therefore shall make you free, ye shall be free indeed (John 8:34–36).

Sin has a way of making us its servant. It enslaves, controls, and dictates our life. Jesus himself breaks the power and control in the lives of us who are his true followers. Only as we repent of sin (turn away from and give it no place), accept Christ's forgiveness, and enter a personal relationship with him, based on his death and resurrection, can we experience freedom from sin.

If we don't have a personal relationship with Christ, we are the servant or slave to sin. As we allow the Holy Spirit to work in our life, it will be evident that **conquering** power is operating in us. I'm not claiming that we will not continue to battle our own flesh and its sinful tendencies. What I am saying is that Christ has set us free from sin's power, and we can live a conquering and victorious life over our sinful nature through yielding to the Holy Spirit.

In water baptism, our being buried under water is in the likeness of Christ being buried in the heart of the earth. Our emerging from the water is an emblem of the resurrection of the Body. In other words, a total change of life; a new life in the Spirit.

Let's understand this. If we have been buried into death, our old man has been crucified. This means our sinful nature was nailed to the cross with Christ. So when Christ rose from the grave unto a new life, this is what is symbolic in water baptism. No, it's not the baptism that makes us a new creature, but the born again experience. We know and understand that. But water baptism symbolizes that we have been given a resurrection in this life. One that should cause us to walk in a newness of life.

> And you hath he quickened, who were dead in trespasses and sins; Wherein in time past ye walked according to

> the course of this world, according to the prince of the power of the air, the spirit that now worketh in the children of disobedience: Among whom also we all had our conversation in times past in the lusts of our flesh, fulfilling the desires of the flesh and of the mind; and were by nature the children of wrath, even as others (Ephesians 2:1–3).

If we are born again, we have been born anew. We have been resurrected. It's a resurrection from death. We who were dead in trespasses and sins, we who walked according to the devil, we who fulfilled the desires of our flesh and mind have been quickened or made alive (Ephesians 2:1). Quickened means that we who were spiritually dead have become alive spiritually.

Water baptism is symbolic of this resurrection from the life of sin. We were dead in our sins, but when we became born again, we were resurrected from a state of deterioration. It was a revival from decay. It was a rising from the dead. Our water baptism is an outward sign of what happened inside. Our old nature died, and we were resurrected to a new life in the Spirit.

Verses eleven through thirteen in our Scripture text sum it all up. How does the resurrected soldier live? We count the old life to be dead and yield the new life to God. We simply reckon ourselves dead unto sin, but alive unto God. We don't give sin an opportunity to reign in our mortal body that we may obey the lusts thereof.

We don't yield our members to unrighteousness. As far as the resurrected soldier is concerned, the old nature no longer exists. It's imperative to understand that living a holy life is our choice. We have been given a free will to choose who or what we yield to.

How do we fight the old man that tries to constantly come back to life and rule? We yield to the Holy Spirit whose reconstructive work is to recreate us from the old nature (first Adam) into the new nature (second Adam who is Christ). We must understand this new life has been resurrected from the life of sin to God. Our yielding to the Spirit and fighting the old man is a form of crucifixion. That's why not many learn to conquer sin. It's much easier to yield to the sinful nature than to crucify, to deny, to reject, etc.

the flesh. Only as we crucify our flesh, can we live as resurrected soldiers free from the power of sin.

In the beginning of this chapter, I stated that Paul reveals that we are to live a holy life and the advantages of such a life. One of the advantages to the resurrected soldier is the freedom from the bondage of sin. As we allow the Holy Spirit to recreate us in the image of Christ, the world will see that sin doesn't have power over us anymore.

Another advantage is that if we live as a resurrected soldier, our lives will bear the fruit of righteousness. As we live a righteous life where sin doesn't have dominion over us, then our life will give glory to Christ.

Living a holy life has many blessings. The main advantage to living a holy life is the freedom from sin and walking in fellowship with God. There's nothing more glorious or advantageous than living in favor with God!

Chapter 11

Walk in the Spirit

If we live in the Spirit, let us also walk in the Spirit.

—GALATIANS 5:25

This I say then, Walk in the Spirit, and ye shall not fulfil the lust of the flesh.

—GALATIANS 5:16

Walking in the spirit seems like a simple admonition or command, but many of God's soldiers have no idea what it means to walk in the Spirit. Yet, the apostle Paul makes clear that only as we walk in the Spirit will we not fulfil the lust of our flesh.

What does it mean to walk in the Spirit? I believe this was somewhat clarified in chapter 9 about the baptism of fire. In order to walk in the Spirit, we must allow the Holy Spirit to do his cleansing work in our life and to do the work in us that God sent him to do.

Unless we fully comprehend the Holy Spirit is God, we will never have an intimate relationship with him. We tend to forget He's the one who dwells within us. He's here to help us live a

Christlike life. It was the Holy Spirit who led Jesus to live a life in conquering power. He prevailed over all He encountered here, and was given the strength of conquering power to suffer the cross.

Too many of God's soldiers are settling for less than what the Holy Spirit desires to do through us, and many are quenching his moving among us. Others of us believe we are walking in the Spirit because the gifts of the Spirit are operating through us. Yet, some of us are afraid of letting him have his way fearing we may lose control.

Walking in the Spirit is the only way to keep us from yielding to our flesh. Jesus, through his life, revealed He did not allow his flesh to control any part of his life. He walked constantly in the Spirit, thereby allowing him to please the Father in all things. Unless we are walking in the Spirit, we cannot please the Father. In other words, if we are not walking under the guidance and direction of the Holy Spirit, we are walking under the guidance and direction of the flesh. If we are in the flesh, we cannot please God (Romans 8:5).

The Holy Spirit doesn't come to us chaotically. He is a divine Person who has a plan and a purpose for our lives. Because God has a plan and purpose for all of us who accept Jesus as Lord and Savior, the Holy Spirit will bring God's will to fruition as we yield to him.

> What? know ye not that your body is the temple of the Holy Ghost which is in you, which ye have of God, and ye are not your own? For ye are bought with a price: therefore glorify God in your body, and in your spirit, which are God's (1 Corinthians 6:19-20).

God's soldiers do not belong to themselves. Once we are born again, we are to give ourselves freely to the Holy Spirit to do God's will in our life. Although He lives or resides in our spirits, his work is limited by what we allow him to do.

That's why we must die to self or our old nature and oblige him to achieve God's purpose in our lives. Our carnal mind is in opposition to the mind of Christ and must be renewed by the Holy Spirit to think his thoughts (Romans 12:2; Philippians 2:5).

If we are going to walk in the Spirit, He has to be permitted to teach us spiritual discernment. Unless the Holy Spirit is leading us, we will not discern the difference between the Holy Spirit, the flesh, or an evil spirit that's influencing us. Only He can help us recognize what is good and evil, what is of God, and what is not. How can we walk with him if we can't discern what is righteous from what is unrighteous? How can we walk with him if we can't discern truth from lies? It's the Holy Spirit who puts a warning in our minds that what we've heard is not quite right. We feel this inward check that something is wrong. Because of those restraints, we are kept from stumbling.

> Let not sin therefore reign in your mortal body, that ye should obey it in the lusts thereof. Neither yield ye your members as instruments of unrighteousness unto sin: but yield yourselves unto God, as those that are alive from the dead, and your members as instruments of righteousness unto God. For sin shall not have dominion over you: for ye are not under the law, but under grace (Romans 6:12-14).

Because Christ has set us free from the power of sin (John 8:36), it no longer has rule over us. The above Scripture exposes that sin tries to reign in us through the desires and lusts of our body or our old nature. We are the ones who decide to yield or not to yield to unrighteousness. Sin does NOT have dominion over us. Through the blood of Christ, we have the power over sin.

Sin has no power over us unless we yield to it. This means we yield our authority over all Satan's power to his power of sin. The Holy Spirit came to deliver us from all the dominion of sin. Whenever we are not living in conquering power, we are not walking in the Holy Spirit.

Let me explain this. Even if we speak in tongues as the evidence of having received the baptism in the Holy Spirit doesn't mean we walk in the Spirit. We are to be the temple of the Holy Spirit and are to glorify God in our bodies and spirit which belong to God (1 Corinthians 6:19-20).

As the temple of the Holy Spirit, we are the dwelling place for the essence of holiness. We must not allow our bodies to be defiled by impurity or evil whether in our actions, our thoughts, our desires, our words, etc. God's Spirit came to make our temple a place of victory over sin. To have the victory, we must walk in the Spirit.

Now, this doesn't mean we will never sin again. However, sin does not have to control us. As we yield to the Holy Spirit, He delivers us from sin. He changes our desires, so we don't want to live the way we did when sin had control over us. Once the Holy Spirit is controlling our desires, He enables us to hate the things God hates.

> The Spirit of the Lord is upon me, because he hath anointed me to preach the gospel to the poor; he hath sent me to heal the brokenhearted, to preach deliverance to the captives, and recovering of sight to the blind, to set at liberty them that are bruised (Luke 4:18).

The anointing Jesus is speaking of is the Holy Spirit. It's an inner anointing now dwelling within us who are born again, and Spirit filled. It's a healing of the Holy Spirit set up inside us to bring healing to the whole man. It heals our physical distresses, brings divine help to our minds, and any part of us that has been injured or bruised. In whatever way we have been wounded, whether physically, mentally, or emotionally, He has our healing.

The Holy Spirit has come in us to bring divine enablement for whatever we may have suffered or experienced in our lives. We must not allow self-pity over emotional injuries or use our past as an excuse for our present failures. If we haven't experienced his healing in certain areas of our lives, perhaps it's because we refuse to forgive. We need to yield to his love and power to free us from the effects of our past that are stifling our present.

As we yield to the Holy Spirit in us, we can conquer our old nature which is prone to sin and grow in Christlikeness. We have to give up our lives to receive his. This takes place as we exchange our old nature at the cross, choosing to die to its sinful ways, and receiving his life. In other words, we choose to decrease and allow him to increase.

As we decrease and He increases, we walk less in the flesh and more in the Spirit. Through this Christlikeness, we will experience conquering power displayed in a greater way in our life. Because we haven't completely yielded to him, his power is suppressed in us. When we walk in the Spirit, we cultivate a dependence on the power of the Holy Spirit who endows us with the power to conquer sin!

Chapter 12

Pentecostal Encounter

And it shall come to pass afterward, that I will pour out my spirit upon all flesh; and your sons and your daughters shall prophesy, your old men shall dream dreams, your young men shall see visions: And also upon the servants and upon the handmaids in those days will I pour out my spirit. And I will shew wonders in the heavens and in the earth, blood, and fire, and pillars of smoke. The sun shall be turned into darkness, and the moon into blood, before the great and terrible day of the Lord come. And it shall come to pass, that whosoever shall call on the name of the Lord shall be delivered: for in mount Zion and in Jerusalem shall be deliverance, as the Lord hath said, and in the remnant whom the Lord shall call.

—JOEL 2:28-32

Before I get into this chapter, I want to address an often time problem with verses thirty-one and thirty-two in Joel chapter 2. Some have problems because those verses were given in such close proximity to the promise of the coming of the Spirit, and yet, it was not fulfilled on the Day of Pentecost.

What we have to remember is the Holy Spirit came at the beginning of the Last Days and the Day of the Lord (Christ's second coming) will come at the end of those days. When things are seen in the proper perspective, the puzzle, problem, or confusion is solved.

The symbolism of the two verses in Joel are put in such a manner to reveal to us just how swift and terrible the judgment of God will be when it comes. God is presented here as a God of judgment. Chapter 3 of Joel shows just how awful the time will be. That's why earlier, I stated that when the day of judgment comes, all second chances are non-existent.

In order to help clarify the separation of the last days to the end, we look at Joel 2:28 that states: *And it shall come to pass **afterward***, whereas, Acts 2:17 states: *And it shall come to pass in the last days.*

In the last days means it's to be a partial and continuous fulfillment during the "Last Days." This was to be a special time for believers. In the Old Testament times, the Holy Spirit came upon certain individuals to enable them to accomplish the task God had given them. Joel foresaw a time when the Spirit's power would be available to ALL believers.

We need to see what happened on the Day of Pentecost was not, in itself, the fulfillment of Joel's prophecy that the Spirit would be poured out upon ALL flesh or all people. The reason that only one-hundred-twenty Jews were filled in the initial outpouring was because the Day of Pentecost was only the beginning of the implementation.

Common sense tells us it was only the beginning, as one-hundred-twenty are a far cry from *all flesh.* Joel made clear when the Holy Spirit came, He would be available to all believers, not just the Jews in the upper room.

All flesh means all believers can be filled. This includes young, old, men, women, boys, girls, slaves, free, educated, uneducated, etc. Simply put, the Holy Spirit is available to all who desire to be baptized in him.

Joel foretold the Spirit's coming would be in abundance. For God to *pour out* his Spirit indicates the Spirit's unlimited availability. Being limitless in its availability means it's not limited in any way to believers. He is not limited to which believer He will fill or how much He will fill each believer.

Joel's prophecy told us the scope of the Spirit's coming. It's not limited to certain believers. Age will not be a factor in receiving the baptism in the Holy Spirit. He will fill the young or old who want him. Male or female will not be a hindrance, for He will fill sons, daughters, men, women, boys, and girls. Position will not be a deterrent. He will come to servants, handmaids, kings, presidents, rulers, etc.

The Holy Spirit baptism is not only for the apostle or prophet, but for the mother or father, the school child, the piano player, the teenager, the nursery schooler, etc. All the people of God or anyone born again can receive the Holy Spirit baptism.

In Acts 1:4, Jesus told the disciples they were not to depart from Jerusalem, but wait for the promise of the Father. Acts 1:5 makes clear the promise is the baptism of the Holy Spirit.

Although the disciples knew they must wait until He came, they didn't understand what it meant. However, they did know God was going to do a special work, or something not done before this time.

Of course, once the Spirit came, it was clear they had a power never experienced by any other believer in God before. Now, the Holy Spirit doesn't merely come upon us, but He comes inside of us and joins himself to our spirit, so that we become one with God.

The filling with the Holy Spirit is called a baptism because it identifies the particular experience we receive. This occurrence is a baptism because it involves us completely. It's a complete immersion where our emotions, mind, and behavior are completely focused and filled by the experience.

So many Christians don't comprehend the baptism in the Holy Spirit is an experience. As our born-again experience gives us such elation at meeting Jesus, the baptism in the Spirit is remarkable. It's as the Apostle Paul stated, "And be not drunk with wine, wherein is excess; but be filed with the Spirit" Ephesians 5:18). It's an incredible enraptured experience of elation. Whereas, being drunk with wine has its negative effects of hangover, etc.

It's imperative to concentrate on the fact that God wants every born again believer baptized with his Spirit. We must realize we are in the days when God is filling his people for his work which must be done.

We cannot effectively do the work of the Lord required in these last days unless we are filled like those on the Day of Pentecost. If God's people didn't need the Holy Spirit baptism today (in the last days), Jesus would not have commanded his followers to wait (not to leave Jerusalem) until they had been baptized in the Holy Spirit.

Peter made clear the experience is for all Christ's followers until He returns. It wasn't just the early church who needed the conquering power. We are just as much in need of it today to overcome. In other words, we are not to start our work for the Lord without the baptism. It's the power enabling us to witness for him and conquer whatever the devil may hurl at us!

Chapter 13

The Conquering Power Within

And when the day of Pentecost was fully come, they were all with one accord in one place. And suddenly there came a sound from heaven as of a rushing mighty wind, and it filled all the house where they were sitting. And there appeared unto them cloven tongues like as fire, and it sat upon each of them. And they were all filled with the Holy Ghost, and began to speak with other tongues, as the Spirit gave them utterance.

–ACTS 2:1-4

In this chapter, we will expound on the fact that the Pentecostal experience is the beginning of a measureless conquering power of the Holy Spirit. We live in the day the Spirit of God is poured forth, and the day of Pentecost was ONLY the beginning of Joel's prophecy being fulfilled.

On that day, the conquering power was poured out. Christ's Church was to be a powerful church enabled to perform the deeds of Christ in his stead. Jesus no longer walks this earth himself. But He walks through us who are his disciples by the indwelling Holy Spirit as He did in the early church.

I have heard it said that the church has been the repository for two thousand years of the most incredible truth in the world, which is the truth about man's need and God's love and grace.

A repository is a place where things are placed for preservation. It's the place that preserves things, so they don't decay, fade away, or become non-existent. However, the problem is the church has kept the truth of man's need and God's love and grace in deep freeze as we would a steak.

If we offer a frozen steak to a hungry person, it's of no practical use to him or her in a cold, hard, frozen state. But if we put the steak on the grill with a fire under it, suddenly the fat starts to sizzle, the juices begin to run, and we begin to smell the aroma of roasting meat. The steak is now accessible to the hungry person.

The Holy Spirit is the vehicle or instrument by which the fire is lit under old truths, so even a non-believer is attracted. I mean, where is this more vividly seen than on the Day of Pentecost? The presence and power of the Holy Spirit was manifested not only by the initial evidence of speaking with other tongues, but the sermon Peter preached resulting in the conversion of three-thousand souls. It was truth on fire, and it moved the hearts of men.

It cannot be overemphasized that the need for the presence and power of the Holy Spirit is just as great today as it was then. The absence of the Spirit's cleansing fire means the failure of the church to fulfill Christ's commission.

This was well articulated by Charles Spurgeon who said, "I think I speak not too strongly when I say that a church in the land without the Spirit of God is rather a curse than a blessing. If we have not the Spirit of God, Christian worker, remember that we stand in somebody else's way; we are a tree bearing no fruit and standing where a fruitful tree might grow."

In the previous chapter, I mentioned God has poured out his Spirit. This means the baptism in the Holy Spirit is unlimited in its availability. Our day is known as the day of the Spirit poured forth.

The Holy Spirit is looking for vessels through whom He may work. What a golden opportunity God's soldiers have to share the Gospel of his power. Do we truly realize that we live in the day of the Spirit poured forth?

We need to ask ourselves if we are as in tune with the Spirit as we need to be. Have we made ourselves as available to him as we should? Are we Christ centered or self-centered? The answer to those questions will determine how much we are available or accessible to the Holy Spirit.

Let me interject a story I heard. I don't remember where, but it is apropos for what we are discussing at present.

> Years ago, in the days of sailing ships, a ship with no steam power was away out at sea. She became becalmed for days, weeks, and months waiting for a breath of wind. The water supply was gone. There was plenty of food, but no water. The sailors were literally dying of thirst. Water was all around them, but not a drop to drink.
>
> Then one day, as they lay exhausted with some already dead, they saw a steamer on the horizon coming toward them. They gathered all the strength they could and ran a signal up the masthead that read: DYING FOR WATER. They were shocked when the steamer changed its course and thought what cruelty.
>
> But the steamer sent a signal back: DIP YOUR BUCKETS. At first, they thought it was devilish and cruel. However, one man said, "Let's try it."
>
> They lowered a bucket into the water and when they pulled it up, the man plunged in his hand, tasted it, and cried, "It's fresh water."
>
> They had drifted into the current of the Amazon. That mighty river is of such quantity that it throws its waters four-hundred miles out to sea before it mingles with the ocean.
>
> They were right in the midst of fresh water, yet, they were dying of thirst.

Do we understand the meaning of this story? We need to dip our buckets and stop blaming God if we are devoid or lacking the conquering power of the Holy Spirit. The mighty river is all about us. If our bucket is full of sin, then it's time to yield to the Spirit and allow him to fill it with his conquering power that will overcome whatever is hindering our being saturated with him.

We are in the days of the Spirit being poured forth. The baptism in the Holy Spirit is unlimited in its availability. This means the Holy Spirit will come to believers without measure. This tells us that we can keep getting more and more and more (unending) of God's Spirit. We are never totally filled, for without measure means it cannot be measured.

No matter how many times after the initial infilling which according to Acts 2:4 is our speaking with other tongues. This initial evidence lets us know we have received the baptism of the Holy Spirit. We receive the Holy Spirit at salvation, but the baptism is given after. There is a big difference from receiving the Spirit at conversion and the baptism of power.

We can be filled continuously and never be filled so much that the Holy Spirit cannot fill us some more. The more we become filled with the Spirit, who cannot be measured or limited, the more transforming and conquering power is bestowed upon us.

The power of the Spirit makes us more than we are and fills us with supernatural energy to conquer the fiercest storms, face mountainous obstacles, and stand firm against any strategies the enemy tries to use against us.

As a Parakletos, the Greek word for comforter, the Spirit becomes our advocate. It's He who stands by as a helper, strengthener, and consoler.

The more we yield to his infilling, He's permitted to become a greater helper, a greater strengthener, a greater comforter, and a greater consoler. As we continuously decrease (deny self) and allow him to increase, He becomes greater and greater in us.

We can never have too much of the Holy Spirit, but we can have too little of him in us. God is still performing signs and wonders today through miracles that affect the personal lives of individuals.

Only as we are filled can we be like the steak on the grill sending forth a sweet savor to the lost of their hungry and needy condition. Furthermore, in the power of the Holy Spirit, a person can do spiritual battle, resist the devil, and be victorious in situations that seem impossible.

Christian, I believe the Lord wants us to question ourselves. "Have we become cold, hard, frozen? Are we thirsty and dry? Have we been baptized in the Spirit with the evidence of speaking in tongues or are we deceived into thinking that it's not for today? Have we depleted the source of the fire in our life?

We need the Spirit to fill us daily and continuously. If we feel cold, hard, frozen, thirsty, and dry, there is a simple solution. First, we need to be baptized in the Spirit. If we have been with the evidence of speaking with other tongues as the Spirit gives utterance, then we need to cry out and ask the Holy Spirit to fill us afresh and anew with his power to conquer all obstacles in this life.

I ask God constantly, "Lord, please fill me afresh and anew with your Holy Spirit. I know I need more of you in my life." It's important to understand that I couldn't go on to do God's will without the constant filling of his Spirit. I cannot overcome this life without his conquering power.

If we are not dwelling in the conquering power of the Holy Spirit, we are walking in the flesh and not the spirit. Walking in the flesh means we have not learned to deny self. Walking in the Spirit means we have conquered our flesh with its lusts.

My prayer for God's soldiers who have read through this book is that we understand the work of the Holy Spirit through his reconstructive work is to recreate us into the image of Christ. We must comprehend that as God the Holy Spirit, He has all the attributes of God. This means the power of God to conquer sin in our life dwells in us through him.

If we desire this power, it's time to get rid of any false doctrines which have filled our mind. We need to have hearts of flesh that yield to the Spirit who can illumine our understanding to the fact that we have become hardened and unteachable. We become obstinate in our belief because it's what our denomination, our preacher, our parents, etc. have taught us. Our belief must be through Holy Spirit revelation and not man's teaching.

Satan has many believing it was only to start the church, the gifts died with the apostles, and we receive the baptism at salvation. The baptism is not the same as receiving the Spirit at conversion. The outpouring at Pentecost was only the beginning. Peter made this clear in his sermon on the day of Pentecost. Presently, the Spirit is still filling those who desire to be filled.

Through a constant infilling of the Holy Spirit, we are enabled to live a life that denies self its lusts of the flesh, the lusts of the eyes, and the pride of life. Without denying self, we encourage our fleshly appetites. If we walk in the spirit, we will NOT fulfill the lusts of the flesh (Galatians 5:16).

The key to abiding in the conquering power of the Holy Spirit is to constantly deny self its carnal appetites. If we're not living in the conquering power of the Spirit, we're walking in the flesh and not the spirit. To walk in the flesh means that we have not learned to deny self. In other words, we cannot walk in the conquering power of the Holy Spirit that defeats sin, unless we deny self and walk in the spirit.

If we yield to the Holy Spirit, we will cultivate lives that produce the fruit of the Spirit. If we yield to the flesh, we will cultivate lives that produce the works of the flesh. We must understand that if we are not being constantly filled with the Spirit, we are being filled with the things that appeal to our carnal nature. His infilling yields righteous living. Our carnal appetites or passions yield unrighteous living. Only as we yield to the Holy Spirit's continuous infilling, will we receive the conquering power to deny self, to overcome sin, and to fulfill God's plan and will for our life!